Over the Hills . . .

The Author

Over the Hills . . .

W. KEBLE MARTIN

MICHAEL JOSEPH * LONDON

First published in Great Britain by
MICHAEL JOSEPH LTD
26 Bloomsbury Street
*London W.C.*1
1968

© 1968 *by W. Keble Martin*

Printed in Great Britain by
Ebenezer Baylis and Son, Ltd.
The Trinity Press, Worcester, and London

To see a world in a grain of sand
And a Heaven in a wild flower,
Hold Infinity in the palm of your hand,
And Eternity in an hour.

William Blake, *Auguries of Innocence*

✳ Contents

✳ Illustrations

Between pages 16 *and* 17

Dr. George Moberly, Headmaster of Winchester College

Mary Anne Moberly, the author's grandmother

The family at Radley College, 1878

A cold winter's day at Dartington Parsonage, 1893

Dartington Parsonage, with the Parish Church in the background

The hall at Dartington Parsonage

The author's sisters, *c.* 1886

The author and his brothers, 1891

Between pages 80 *and* 81

Keble Martin watching birds at Dartington, *c.* 1897

Dartington Parsonage

Thanks are due to the following for permission to reproduce photographs in which they hold the copyright: *Devon News Service, Exeter* frontispiece; *Express & Echo Exeter* facing page 113; *Postmaster General* facing page 144, bottom.

The drawings in this book appear with the kind permission of George Rainbird Limited with the exception of that on page 146 for which thanks are due to the Woodbury News Committee. All plate references in the text refer to *The Concise British Flora.*

PEJUS LETHO FLAGITIUM

❋ FAMILY MOTTO

Pejus Letho Flagitium—Worse than death is disgrace.

We have always been somewhat moved by this family motto.

The character of a native flower is very dependent on the kind of seed from which it has grown, and upon the soil in which it is rooted. Here then is the seed and the soil.

My father Charles Martin was a son of William Martin, Rector of Staverton on the River Dart in South Devon. This William Martin had walked across Staverton Ford and married Jane Champernowne, daughter of Arthur Champernowne of Dartington Hall. (The writer as a small boy knew this lady well and sometimes played backgammon with her.) The principal family home was Overbury Park in Gloucestershire where three successive generations had provided Members of Parliament for Tewkesbury. The Martins were a large family of which one branch was prominent in the banking world. William Martin, my grandfather, had brothers: Joseph at Ham Court near Tewkesbury, George the lawyer, Chancellor of Exeter Diocese, Henry in 44th Foot Reg. at Waterloo, and Richard, Vicar of Menheniot. My father's brother Richard was Vicar of Ilfracombe and Sub Dean of Exeter Cathedral; his brother Harington was a captain in the Navy.

After I was ordained and engaged in humble parochial work, I received a request to contribute to the restoration of St. George's Chapel at Windsor. I sent my humble contribution promptly, and to my surprise later on received a beautiful certificate, saying that I was a descendant of a Knight of the Garter and that my name had been inscribed on the Roll of Benefactors at St. George's Chapel at Windsor, so it is there today. This certificate was deliberately hidden for many years and then framed and hung, as it might be some inspiration to my family who were becoming grown up.

My father used to go by horse coach from South Devon to Winchester, and at Winchester College he became in due course Prefect of Hall, i.e. Head boy, and he married Dora Moberly, a younger daughter of George Moberly the Head-master of Winchester, afterwards Bishop of Salisbury. Thus the Head Boy married the Headmaster's daughter, but had to wait till he was 29 before he could afford to marry. The wedding took place on Holy Cross Day, 14 September 1869, at St. Mary's, Brighstone in the Isle of Wight, because for a short period her father, George Moberly, was Rector of Brighstone between his time at Winchester and the Bishopric of Salisbury. So when my mother was collecting her wedding trousseau, her father was getting ready his episcopal robes. He was consecrated Bishop that autumn. My mother there-fore belonged to another family of which many were hard-working clergy or wives of clergy. In the Winchester days, George Moberly and his family always spent the school holi-days at Field House in Hursley. He was for many years one of the most intimate friends of John Keble, Rector of Hursley, a leader of the Oxford Movement. And George Moberly's children, including my mother, often went to play at Hursley Rectory. My mother had happy recollections of this. The mutual correspondence of George Moberly and John Keble was published in *Dulce Domum*. It is odd that my second god-father was Philip Champernowne, a cousin on my father's side whose mother was a daughter of Tom Keble of Fairford, a niece therefore of John Keble.

My father became a classical scholar of New College, Oxford. From there, after a short period as a master at

Harrow School, he became a lecturer on Greek Philosophy at Christ Church, Oxford. During that time he was ordained. And in 1869 he became Warden, i.e. Headmaster of St. Peter's College, Radley, so his portrait hangs in Radley College dining hall. I was born at Radley, 9 July 1877, but remember nothing of Radley. Those were the days of big domestic staff, and I was often told the story that shortly before we left, the butler came in one day during luncheon to apologize: "I am very sorry, madam, but the pudding has gone up the chimney."

So a long life started in beautiful and happy surroundings, and that happy confidence which comes from faithful Christian teaching and example in family life. We were reminded that our parents prayed for us. And that saying is true: "Unto whom much is given, of him shall much be required." The Christian faith was unquestioned at this stage. The whole household attended family prayers and heard the Scriptures read.

My father as a schoolmaster taught us to work hard, and often, when we wanted something unsuitable he replied: "Wanting has nothing to do with it", and he knew what was best for us. In 1879 my father left his school and college work in order to do Church work in a country parish like John Keble, but adding to this the training or coaching of young men for the University, usually two or three pupils who lived in the Rectory. In those days there was special scope for this arrangement.

So we came first to Wood Norton with Swanton, near East Dereham in Norfolk.

One of my earliest recollections at the age of 5 years is that of joining my elder brothers and sisters by the light of a candle outside our parents' bedroom door very early on Christmas morning, singing a roundelay:

"May God bless all friends dear with a Merry Merry Christmas, and a Happy New Year

> May God bless all friends dear with a Merry Merry Christmas
> May God bless all friends dear"

and the parents coming out to greet the children. Another of my earliest recollections was at about 5 years of age sitting alone at a writing-table, gazing at white cloud billows sailing in deep blue sky; I wondered much at this. There was a large garden and a shrubbery with bluebells, where we each had our little garden bed to look after. There was a Rectory farm and much milk was given away to village children who came daily to fetch it, and I meanly disapproved of a little boy picking the beautiful mauve crocus flowers as he passed. My education began—my mother told me to let him have some for his mother. A large fir-tree spread its lower branches on the ground beside the lawn, and an early recollection is that of discovering that a duck had a cosy nest and eggs in the long grass under one of the branches. My eldest brother made me very astonished showing me six thrushes' nests built, he said, one on top of the other. It was not until some years later that it dawned on me that he had put them there. For an outing, we were taken to see rhododendrons in some woods called Fulmodeston Severals. I was given some geraniums to grow in my garden bed at the end of the summer of, I think, 1883. I was 6 years of age. I lifted these geraniums into a box as we were to move house. I wept because, of course, the removers did not go down the shrubbery to fetch them, and they were left behind.

We moved to Poulshot Rectory near Devizes. Soon after we moved to Poulshot, probably in 1884, we were in the wagonette in Devizes. I was alone with my father at the moment. And he wanted to go into the Bank (Midland probably) in the Market Place. I was nearly 7 years old. He handed me the reins and said: "Now hold them tight, hold them tight." I was always keen to do what he wanted, but misunderstood. I gripped the reins and tugged at them for all I was worth. The horse backed the wagonette on to the pavement, and was just bumping against the windows of the Bank, before I discovered what was happening. My father darted out of the Bank and put things right. At Devizes we were within easier reach of Salisbury, to which some of us were taken sometimes by train to see my grandfather Bishop Moberly. In 1884 we went for Palm Sunday. I remember being impressed by the stately Cathedral and being taken to see the great palms near the high altar. We played about in the Bishop's residence. I remember watching the lighting of the chandeliers each with a large number of candles, lighted with a candle in a long rod in the drawing-room, and then later going to play for a few minutes in the Bishop's study to find a secret door in the book-case before going to bed. In hot summer weather we set off to Salisbury at 6 o'clock in the morning, that is by wagonette to Devizes Station, three miles away.

At Poulshot Rectory there was an enormous plane-tree too near the house. It was so tall that it was visible from Potterne, a village five miles away, standing above elms and oaks. The stem was enormous. It was a danger to be removed. So when the sap was running one spring it was cut down. I remember Jim Pearce catching bowls full of crimson sap. Just think: in spring, by a little chemical action, I suppose, called osmosis, water is injected into the root hairs, producing such a pressure as to force the sap through the wood tissues up 120 feet to expand the leaves in spring, each leaf of perfect construction and circulation. What is the pressure per square inch in the wood tissues? Nature is wonderful. This is happening all around us this springtime.

We were a big family and three boys in the middle of the family were much together. I had three elder brothers, and had no chance of becoming conceited. A kind uncle, Edward Moberly, often stayed with us. He was musical and the conductor of the Avon Vale Orchestra. He started my sisters' training in the violin, in which they became very proficient.

And he fitted up the boys with all that was needed for collecting butterflies and moths, nets, setting boards, store boxes and even cages for rearing them from caterpillars. For this purpose it was necessary to find the correct food plants. This led to the earliest effort to know some wild plants. What fun we had chasing some butterfly, because we thought it new to us, sometimes across the garden crops to the annoyance of the gardener. In the evening we "sugared" the trees as an attraction to moths, especially two beautiful tulip trees on the lawn. It was a life full of interest and activity. We had our little garden plots to cultivate and were already learning to play tennis out of domestic schoolroom hours.

At Poulshot Rectory beyond the lawn there was a sunken hedge to lengthen the view, and then a field of five acres with corncrakes and skylarks and yellow meadow wagtails. This field or the six-acre one beyond, was usually laid up for mowing. In this case at sunrise on a midsummer morning, when it was wet with dew, five men mowed with scythes, starting from the left, each a yard or two in front of the one on his right. It was five scythes together in echelon across the big field and back again, sometimes deliberately missing a nest of skylark or corncrake, with occasional stops for scythe whetting or for liquid refreshment. Soon the five or six acres were mown and waiting to be tossed by hand, in which we all helped. There were no machines.

The same kind relative mentioned above gave us also a good archery set, targets, bows and arrows, but we were dangerous boys together. When we became a little proficient in target practice, we took the bows and arrows down the Glebe fields, letting them fly at pigeons and starlings in the tree tops, without looking to see that there was nothing in the field beyond. In due course on retrieving the arrows we found that one was stuck in the thick hide of a big pig. We tried to drive it into a shed. Have you ever tried to drive a pig in an open field? It would be quicker if you were feeding the brute. However, we succeeded at last, and apparently the

Dr. George Moberly,
Headmaster of Winchester
College, later Bishop of
Salisbury, the author's
grandfather; from a painting
by F. Grant, R.A.

Mary Anne Moberly, the
author's grandmother; from
a painting by Sir David
Wilkie. She said she would
never have worn this hat if
the artist had not persuaded
her to put it on

The family at Radley
College, 1878: The Rev.
Charles and his wife, Dora
Martin—the author's
parents; with (*left to right*)
Dora, Charlie, Keble (on
mother's knee), Jack, Arthur
(*on father's knee*) and Edith

A cold winter's day at
Dartington Parsonage, 1893.
The author is on the right
in a Marlborough College
cap

Dartington Parsonage, with
the Parish Church in the
background

The hall at Dartington
Parsonage

The author's sisters, *c.* 1886.
Left to right: Katharine,
Edith, Nellie, Dora

The author and his brothers,
1891. *Left to right:* Jack,
Keble, Charlie, Dick, Arthur

arrow was only in the hide and had done no real harm. But it was a lesson. (At a much later date, when rabbits were a plague, we invited a learned friend to come and shoot them while we were ferreting. For this purpose we usually stand near the fence and shoot along it or from it, but our friend would insist on standing 40 yards out and firing at the hedge, when another gun, my son, was the other side of it!)

But to return to Poulshot, those were happy days for us as boys. The surroundings were so natural and normal and healthy. Nature seemed to display itself and co-operate. We had lots to do. My father had some financial anxiety caused chiefly by the payment of school fees and maintaining nine children. But we learned cabinet making at school, including the making of egg cabinets and insect cabinets. These important items were home made, including one large enough to hold 600 or more moths and butterflies, duly cork-lined and veneered with mahogany. It took three years to make and it was finished at Dartington. It is still quite full, with a very beautiful collection which took 15 years to make. We rarely bought anything. However, we did manage to purchase a little yellow book called *Insect Hunter's Companion*, not like a young schoolfellow who, I believe, bought one called *Advice to Young Moth-ers*! We had beautiful moths around us. Eyed hawk-moths bred annually on willows near the house at Poulshot. And large red-underwings used to spread themselves in daylight on an old brick wall, where they were hard to see. Leopard moths and many others. But especially I think of the birds. There were yew-trees near the house in which golden crested wrens always nested. We watched them, and one day when the young birds were leaving the nest we saw nine young gold crests, tiny birds, sitting in a row on a twig being fed, a truly pretty sight. Sometimes in the early morning, we have watched the gold crests building their nest under a yew twig or under the end of a spruce fir branch, apparently winding cobwebs and thin grasses round the twigs to suspend the nest: one bringing materials and the other building, in

true partnership. Lesser whitethroats arrived in summer and
built a thin nest of goose grass in some snowberry bushes
opposite the dining-room window, two eggs of this were preserved to prove identity. At the end of the kitchen garden a
Church day school was built of brick (to this a little sanctuary
was added for Sunday evensongs and daily mattins, as it was
more in the village than the parish church). For some reason,
on the garden front of the school two bricks were missing
about 4 feet from the ground, and there was a nice hollow
inside. We watched robins building a nest in it. Then a pair
of redstarts arrived and contributed to the nest and sometimes drove off the robins. In due course one robin's egg was
laid. Next day it was rolled out on to the plaster and one
blue redstart's egg was in the nest. Then we went back to
school; I wonder which won.

But I could be a horrid little boy at about 11 years old.
One evening after dusk when moth hunting was rather dull,
a hedgehog ran blindly towards me along the path. I put the
butterfly net in front of it and caught it. Then I took it in
the net to the party in the drawing-room, where there were
visitors, two sisters. I deposited the hedgehog in the lap of
the younger sister, Agatha Kestell-Cornish, whose father and
brother were in succession Bishops of Madagascar. My father
could be stern sometimes! In later experience we sometimes
fed the hedgehogs with bread and milk on the lawn, and they
occasionally ran under our windows at midnight grunting
merrily.

At Poulshot the wasps learned to go into the larder, and
if the door was shut they found their way out through the
keyhole carrying fragments of ham with which to feed their
grubs (or so we always believed).

At Poulshot there were ponds in the corners of the fields
for watering cattle and these provided a home for water-hens.
A large pond beside the field nearest to the house also provided skating in winter, and what winters we had! In the last
Christmas holidays there, 1890/91, the ice was 18 inches

thick. The thermometer registered 32 degrees of frost on many nights. We had for three weeks in January (1891) an ice igloo on the tennis court. The snow had a hard crust and we skated on it from the house to the pond. I was a younger brother and then took a pride in getting home from skating before the others to make a big dining-room fire for them and lots of hot toast for tea. In early February 1895, the ice was again 18 inches thick, and as one of the older boys at Marlborough, I was allowed to go by train to skate on Swindon reservoir. The M. & S.W. railway had wooden benches only in 3rd Class and at least in our compartment no glass to middle windows which were therefore open even in the hardest frost. But I am anticipating. This was in school days.

* SCHOOL DAYS

We were just ordinary average boys like thousands of others, learning to be humble, none of us were distinguished as scholars or as athletes.

When we were small we began our education under a governess at home. I was called Billy in those days and my brother, Arthur, next older than myself at 10 years old was declared by his sisters to be "a bother to Mother, a tease to Billy and a plague to us". So he was packed off to a boarding school. This was Eton House at Aldeburgh on Sea. Similarly, I was sent there before my tenth birthday. This was the summer of 1887 and of Queen Victoria's first Jubilee. In the short hours of darkness the windows in the town were illuminated with candles arranged in the pattern of V.R. The shingle came up at that time to the walls of the Town Hall.

And the bonfire was made on the shingle to the north of the town, and I always said it was made on a precious clump of sea-pea. Whether this is true or not I cannot say. We went for nice walks along the coast and Aldeburgh gave us a first introduction to abundant seaside flowers.

Arriving home for the first time from school I was much excited. My brothers got out of the wagonette on to the white dusty road as it spun along the village green at Poulshot in order to take a short cut. I was not to be beaten. I stood on the back door of the wagonette and jumped off. The next thing I remember was the doctor, Carless, fetched on horseback from three miles away, standing over me saying, "He'll be all right, he's coming round."

For the Summer Term 1888 I went alone to St. Michael's School, Lyme Regis. There were other sons of clergy there. Young boys do need occupation out of school hours. I took a prominent part in digging a deep pit in the small garden, where we could get under and hide—most dangerous. For swimming lessons we were put on our "tummies" on benches and taught a swimming stroke, then taken out to a boat just out of our depth and pushed in. The master made rather free use of the cane. In the autumn I had measles badly. My bed was next to the fireplace in a crowded bedroom. I was feverish and kicked all the bedclothes off and then fell on my head on the stone hearth and saw a bright ring of stars which I never forgot. A week later I was caned severely for not working hard enough. It was horrid but I probably worked harder when the soreness was passed. I was not conscious of any crime, but in these days when boys really do sin with their bodies, they should surely suffer in their bodies. A good caning every Monday morning would do good. After a first experience the prospect would be a good deterrent, I am sure.

Early in 1889 the school moved to the Old Rectory at the top of Lyme Regis. And in the first Lent Term there I had influenza and, with two other boys, was rather neglected in an attic; the domestic staff sometimes forgot our meals. There happened to be a bad fire in the lower part of the street. We got out of bed and peeped at it. Bishop John Wordsworth of Salisbury was there for a confirmation, staying in a hotel opposite the fire. The schoolboy story was that he joined the firefighters with a bucket and went in too far, and had to be pulled out by his heels. Anyway, Mrs. Wordsworth found her way up to see us in the attic. She was most motherly and got us better attended to. There was a nice old garden which was out of bounds to us, but in the following spring I saw a thrush visiting a bush in it. So one morning I went out before breakfast and got over the railing and ran across to look at it. I saw the four beautiful blue eggs with dark spots. It was quite worth the risk, but it was right in front of the windows, if any master had seen me it meant another caning. I was really learning more about birds at home at Poulshot. But we were sometimes allowed to go for walks in the landslip area with butterfly nets or to birds nest. I remember seeing a weasel with a small mouse in its mouth. The slim creature stood erect on its hind legs looking at us with the little dead mouse in its mouth intended doubtless for the baby weasels. I never had more than a few pence of pocket money and could not usually buy anything, but in 1889 I went shares with another boy in making, I believe, my first purchase. We bought a pair of blue rock pigeons for a few pence. We made a nice nesting-box, fastened it to a tree in our part of the grounds. We kept them in for a bit to make them at home. We fed them assiduously but it was too near the bushes and a cat got one and the other had to be sadly returned to the loft it came from. At the end of that Summer Term, just after my twelfth birthday I proudly asked for a whole ticket at Salisbury but had not enough money to pay for it. I was only small and was told I must travel with a half ticket and felt very humiliated. We never had pocket money enough to buy anything, but were none the worse for that.

In the Autumn Term 1889 I was sent to Wayneflete, Clifton, an excellent school under a Wykehamist, the Rev.

J. H. Wilkinson, in a wonderful large building. I learned more there. There were some boys in my dormitory who were too bossy, and there was quite a bit of wrestling in consequence, but we learned to respect one another and parted good friends. Out of school on wet days we did a lot of roller skating in a very large basement corridor and round the gymnasium, learning caution against colliding in the doorway. We had a good playing field, and when I won a hundred yards race, the prize was a cricket ball, and I made an effort to hide my disappointment; I was never a keen cricketer. But I was allowed to go after butterflies to the Leigh Woods with my cousin Bertie Moberly, (later in the Army a Major-General). That was across the Clifton Suspension Bridge, where we floated empty paper bags away on the breeze. It was at Wayneflete that I watched the great blizzard (Feb. 22, 1891) which did so much damage in Devon, when my people had just moved to Dartington. We were still at school for that early Easter, and on Good Friday I was really shocked to see on Durdham Down all the apparatus of a Bank Holiday, swings, merry-go-rounds and entertainments of all sorts, a glimpse of a different life. One day in the summer holidays that year, my father was to be specially busy at home, and wanted us out of the way, and the horse wanted exercising so my brother and I aged 15 and 14 were sent off with the groom to a certain place with butterfly nets, and we, knowing little about it, caught a pair of large blues, which are very rare and should not be captured. They are still in the cabinet.

For the Autumn Term of 1891 I went to Marlborough College, and was there for four years, starting in the junior house. I walked on Sundays at first with a friend Hugh Raven, who left early for medical training. The first class I attended was taken by the bursar, old Mr. Thomas, in the gymnasium, as classroms were very inadequate at that time. In the summer of 1892 we celebrated the Jubilee of the school, my brother Arthur came with a Volunteer detachment from Winchester who were keeping their quincentenary. We played Rugby football in autumn and hockey on the Commons in the Lent Term. One day in football I collared my opposing three-quarters, and another bigger boy a forward, also turned and collared my man. Our heads met behind his back. And when I recovered consciousness a fair-haired boy was tenderly surrounding me with sweaters beside the pitch. He was good to me and got me to the school doctor, who pulled my broken nose into place without an anaesthetic! The boy was Oscar Watkins, son of the Archdeacon of Delhi. He became a faithful friend, and we went for many Sunday walks in the Savernake Forest together. About a year later another boy, H., not knowing that we were friends, asked me to be his (H.'s) second in a fist fight. He was going to fight Watkins after breakfast behind the cricket pavilion. So this resulted in the first peacemaking job I ever did. I soon discovered that if a new boy arrived, and another boy was asked by a mutual friend to look after him, it was wiser not to tell the new boy this, but to quietly look out for opportunities of showing friendly kindness.

I was in due course removed to Mr. B.'s house. Mr. B. was now my housemaster. He was reputed to be an Italian teaching French. I was to be prepared for Confirmation, and the rule was that the housemaster prepared candidates for Confirmation. Mr. B.'s instruction was read aloud from a manuscript written by Dr. Bell, the headmaster. Not a very suitable arrangement, but I had my father as a background, and old Bell took us himself for the last class. And the instruction given in this strange way brought wonderful conviction of Christian truth. Before my Confirmation, my godfather, Willie Awdry, whose wife was my mother's sister, rode over from Salisbury on a push-bike. He lost his way in the dark and, feeling his way into a farm, found he was holding a donkey's tail. He duly arrived the next day. Later he became Bishop of Tokyo, and wanted me to join him in Japan.

The moral standard of our house at Marlborough might have been better but was fairly good. A former head boy of the house, Ferguson-Davie, later Bishop of Natal, came back and took house prayers and bore a strong Christian witness. This made a great impression on us. I was a three-quarter back in Rugby football, and when a big boy behaved in a disgusting manner, even I succeeded in stopping it by collaring him round the legs, and with a great heave throwing him. He did not try it again. There was a milestone outside the College gate, on some days we had to run to the first milestone and back. I was zealous and often ran to the second, trying to keep up with the horses.

The Natural History Society of the School was very active, and was well run by Mr. Meyrick, an authority on moths and butterflies. He took us for good field days in the summer. I remember going into morning school with a butterfly net hidden, and running at 12 o'clock to the Savernake Forest with another boy for interesting butterflies and back to 1.30 luncheon in a state of perspiration. This was in July and sunny weather. During school days we were kept well in touch with our home as my mother wrote nice letters to us all with great regularity, almost every week.

✳ VOLUNTEERS

In those early days young boys thought that they were called to fill a small place in that great beneficent and Christian institution, the British Empire. There was a keen spirit of loyalty then. So at Marlborough we joined the Volunteers, a defensive organization, and we persevered in rifle practice. The motto of the Volunteers was "To preserve Peace, be prepared for War". I was in the school rifle eight, competing with other schools at Bisley for the Ashburton Shield. We also went each summer to camp at Aldershot. The camp was on that wet Laffans Plain where large gentians grew in the marsh. And strange as it may seem, we were allowed to take our service rifles and ammunition home by train for practice in the holidays. At Dartington we had short ranges in two quarries on the glebe with reduced duplicates of service targets. And as there were three Volunteers in the family my brothers challenged any three of the Totnes Volunteers to a match on their range, beside the River Dart. I was not up to standard then (1894) and we were beaten, which was good for us. I may refer to the rifle practice again later. Latterly there was a real happiness in returning to school at Marlborough, because I had good friends there.

In the summer holidays of 1894 or '95, we heard of a wonderful cavern at Pridamsleigh Farm on the east side of the River Dart nearly opposite Buckfast. Three boys decided to explore it. We had only heard of the wonders of Kents Cavern, Torquay. Having no other kind of light we took three new candles. After walking through many passages we realized that we did not know the way out again. So we agreed to hunt for it with one candle only, putting out the others. We could not easily find the way out. We had only one inch left of the last candle when we found it, so we did not leave our bones there. We went again, trailing 500 yards of white cotton to lead us back to the entrance. Candles were the only light, and every evening at home ten bedroom candlesticks were on a tray, with a tiny oil lamp to light them at, in order to light us to bed.

Some of my friends left Marlborough before me and I was leaving at the end of the Summer Term, July 1895. The railway connection for South Devon was very poor, and I thought I could catch an earlier train at Swindon. The College gates opened at 5 a.m. that day. So I set off laden with a bag in one hand and overcoat and cricket bat in the other, to walk quickly to Swindon G.W. Station for the 8 a.m. train. It was hot. I hurried but I just managed to see that train leaving the platform without me. It was 12 miles and the porter at the gate reminded me recently that "it is still 12 miles".

＊ DARTINGTON EARLY YEARS

In February 1891 my father had become Rector of Dartington near Totnes, South Devon, where Hurrell Froude, a friend of John Keble, had been Rector, and on 22 February, when some roof repairs were in progress at the Rectory, there was a terrible blizzard of snow. It was 3 feet deep in the open fields, lanes were mostly 6 feet deep. There were great drifts on Dartmoor, burying cottages over the chimney pots. There were, I believe, twelve trains snowed up in Devon. Many people trying to return home from work, failed to battle against the depth of snow and were found several days later. The snow was followed by heavy rain. And the floods were so great that many sheep from Dartmoor were entangled in the upper branches of oaks beside the River Dart, and the fleece was there all the summer following. The oak woods in some cases were a sad sight, with many big limbs broken down to the ground. In our Parsonage copse there were tall 25–30 feet laurels beside some of the paths, and these were laid with their great stems plaited across the paths. As boys we set to work in the holidays to cut them out. It took us more than two years and we came back to this work each school holiday time. We kept the paths clear of bracken and brambles at all times. At the entrance to Parsonage copse there was a nice shrubbery (a recent visit showed me that it is changed completely now) with three picturesque grottoes and a butter well, where the butter was hung in the water surface for cooling, and a nice summer-house where the tree creepers always nested behind loose bark. I had a secret path in the laurels near some box bushes, where the dormice slept all through the winter. They were tightly curled up in their nests with the long tail curled over the head and right round the body.

In autumn the woods were quiet and peaceful with just the voice of a robin. One early morning I saw a tug of war on a woodland path, a dormouse and a long-tailed field mouse both had hold of a hazel-nut. There were a lot of hazels, and the nuts were in much demand. The nuthatches stored them in some old hollow trees, and the squirrels carried them out to the pastures, and buried them under some tussock or a dock plant. We have seen them go out in two inches of snow, scratch it away, and find the nut without fail. These were, of course, the red squirrels, the grey squirrel had not yet been imported.

There were such a lot of red squirrels. We enjoyed seeing them, running up the tree in jerks and stopping to cough at us. One day I peeped into a chaffinch's nest in a laurel bush, moss and lichen lined with hair. There was one egg, then I saw a squirrel coming across the wood, out to the ends of the oak branches on to the bending twigs, jumping to the twigs of the next tree and so across the wood, finally running down a stem and on to the laurel, straight to the chaffinch's nest (he knew it was there), taking it quickly in his mouth, tipping the egg out right in front of my nose, then taking the nest up the stem and back across the wood to the drey in the top of a tall holly for his mate to line the drey with. Another day a squirrel came out of a nest and went hunting. It was early summer. I thought there might be babies so I climbed up quickly to have a look at them, and failing to get my hand in through the horizontal sticks, I opened the top of the nest with the one available hand, but I got such a sharp nip from mother squirrel that I never saw those babies. The baby squirrel's tail is long and rather dormouse-like at first with its short fur.

The red squirrels seemed to do no harm, unlike the grey one which nibbles the lower bark, and may kill the tree. The red squirrel supplements his food in winter by nibbling the uppermost twigs of ash and perhaps of oak. In our glebe woods alone we must have usually had about six or eight pairs of red squirrels, with dreys in all the tall hollies. We enjoyed seeing them. But now the native oaks and ash are gone, and holly and the red squirrels are gone, and I often ask myself, "What is the fate of the smaller fauna and flora in this change to conifers?"

The writer was not alone. He had four brothers and four sisters whose example and co-operation had an important influence upon him. We were a large, happy family brought up in Christian tradition.

The eldest, Edith, went off early to earn her living, so as not to be a burden at home. She was a court dressmaker in London, and was a keen church member all her life. She kept a very convenient open house for her brothers and sisters, when they had to be in London for study or business, or passing through to France in the First World War.

The second sister, Dora, was a keen water-colour artist, a member of the Pandora Sketching Club. We were occasionally with her, bird-watching while she sketched. The pictures are widely scattered now. She played the violincello in the family orchestra. Dora kept house for one relative after another, for me on one occasion, for her brother Charlie at Hampton, before he was married, for her Uncle Walter Moberly, Vicar of Sydenham for about nine years, and for others. She was a good angel in time of need.

The next two sisters, Nellie and Katharine, were good violin players. As a family at Dartington we often listened to good music in the longer evenings. Musical friends from

Ermington sometimes joined them. This was the family orchestra, the real thing, long before radio-music was invented. Later on they played in the Cathedral Orchestra at Exeter for some years. Nellie joined my lodging at Beeston, teaching the Vicar's daughter for a time. Katharine had many music pupils, whom we still sometimes meet.

Of the brothers, Charlie, the eldest, was a fruit grower, especially on a large scale for Lord Sudely at Toddington in Gloucestershire, where he directed the planting of more than a thousand acres of fruit right up the Cotswold Hills, above the normal frost line. He was much sought after as an adviser in fruit growing. He was very hospitable to us after I was married. We visited him on annual holidays and made the acquaintance of the flora of the oolite soil of the Cotswold Hills and the beech woods and their orchids.

The second brother, Jack, was a kind elder brother to me when I was small. After taking his degree at Oxford he went into the Fairfield Shipbuilding Co. at Glasgow. But he was so shocked by his fellow workers that after a year there he gave it up. He offered himself for ordination and went to Cuddesdon Theological College. Later he did good work in several parishes. He became Rector of Dartington and finally of Holwell in Oxfordshire. We had visited him at Simonsbath Rectory on Exmoor as well as at Dartington.

The next brother, Arthur, was trained in London as an architect. In the first war he served for two years on the La Bassée Canal. After the war he was on the staff of the Royal Military College and rebuilt the Chapel at Sandhurst, a beautiful work. He built some churches in the South London area and St. Luke's Church, Milber, after the writer's dream. He was architect to the Duchy of Cornwall and to Lord Clinton's estates in Devon. He was a C.V.O. and co-operated often with the writer, planning parochial buildings.

The younger brother, Dick, was trained in engineering at the Central Technical College. He first surveyed the Angola railway for the Portuguese Government in a dry desert area of South West Africa, among lions and big snakes, living only in tents. He brought back a butterfly collection, which we took together to the Natural History Museum. He was afterwards for a long while Chief Engineer to the South Indian Railway based on Trichinopoly. His family living mostly at Ootacamund. Finally he came to live in Exmouth and was Treasurer for the Milber Church Appeal Fund, which he helped much. One of his daughters lives in Exton, where I minister, and is often helpful to me.

But to return to the life at Dartington, by day we were cutting woodland paths or mowing the big lawns with hand mower. We played tennis quite a lot. We went in summer holidays to the Parsonage boat-house over a mile away and up the river for a picnic, often at Folly Stickle where the tall Indian balsam had been introduced. In wet weather we worked in the domestic carpenter's shop. We had learned cabinet making at school and worked on at the insect cabinet. On fine summer mornings we sometimes went to bathe in the River Dart, three-quarters of a mile away at Stillpool above Staverton Ford. The pool was reputed to be very deep. We were told you could sink a church tower in it. There was a nice rock to dive from. Young kingfishers used to chase one another in circles over the water or a dipper would sing with full rich notes. We ran back in time to ring the church bell for 8 o'clock daily mattins for my father.

Dartington was my home during the period 1891–99, that is for holidays from school and vacations from Oxford, but also for a year between school and college (August '95– September '96). My father was Rector till 1910, and my brother Jack later. There were many happy experiences of the birds almost every day and records were kept of the first singing and nesting of resident species and the arrival, nesting and departure of migratory kinds. It was after these elaborate records that my friend Colonel Studdy proposed me as a member of the British Ornithologists' Union to which I belonged for some years, but owing to financial stringency in early married life, I could not pay my subscription. I lost my membership; I was also too busy to attend to it.

Speaking of birds, at Dartington, in the summer holidays or about the beginning of July when foliage has become dense, I would go into the wood and a flock of young tits nearly always surrounded me. They came quite close and looked at me, as if to inspect the intruder. These were nearly all young birds, without full adult colour. Great tits, blue tits, cole tits and long tails, but usually in July and August a wonderful silence settles upon the woods. Later in the season the flocks of birds develop. And any morning in mild weather in late autumn and winter I would find a sheltered place to stand, and wait for the call of the nuthatch. The nuthatch is the only one that is apt to move head downwards on the stems. He has a clear whistle. He comes leading the normal community of small resident birds, hunting through the leaf-less trees for food, often three or four dozen of them. These include all the five common titmice with treecreepers and the goldcrests which keep mostly to the scattered spruce. Some-times lesser spotted woodpeckers came also for company. The birds are too busy to talk much. But they seem to be a community that trust one another and the nuthatch's call. Every time he whistles there is a general move forward. This is a daily occurrence. Towards spring they talk more. The treecreeper in spring going up a stem in jerks puts his head on one side to say "Tiddley, Widdeley, Widdeley wee" up-wards on the last syllable, or the goldcrest sings a little with a tiny mouse-like voice.

A spruce fir touched the window of the room where I worked and goldcrests were often at very close quarters, even within 3 feet of me. It is impossible to put a bird's song on paper. But I should bear witness that the song of the woodlark is specially attractive, sometimes singing even at night, floating peacefully over the tree tops or over the house: Tee, teedle, eedle, eedle, eedle, ee; talee, talee, talee, talee, talee; twiddle, twiddle, twiddle, twiddle, twiddle, twiddle, the semicolon represents the spacing of the soft sweet notes. We had lots of nests, including missel-thrush, jays and wood-pigeons, the last of course with two eggs only. We sometimes recited the rhyme: "The Woodpigeon says 'Coo Coo. I can only bring up two!' As for the little Jenny Wren he can safely bring up ten, and make them all little gentlemen."

The woodpeckers were entertaining. The green wood-pecker with his crimson head is our British anteater, scattering the ants' nest, and pecking them up. We watched them cutting a nesting hole in a poplar, which is soft wood. Nut-hatches sometimes made the last year's hole smaller with mud for their own nest; but if a starling spotted it before the mud was hard, he would steal the hole for his nest. At a later date the greater spotted woodpecker (black and white and scarlet) entertained the family at Gidleigh by pecking mag-gots out of old elm poles in front of our window daily at breakfast time, another pair brought up a family just outside my bedroom window at Yarner; they were in poplar too.

The crows were rascals. The poultry at Dartington had a free run and generally did well on it, but they sometimes made a nest on the hedge-bank of a near orchard. A crow would sit on an apple-tree and wait till the hen came off cackling with joy over another egg laid. The crow popped down, drove his bill through the egg, and so carried it to his nest in a big spruce fir in the neighbouring wood to feed his family. The ground below this nest was thickly strewn with the egg-shells.

In the autumn of 1895 we went bird-watching at Slapton Ley. This was a 21-mile run on a push-bike and we were fortunate in being there on several calm days. There were real crowds of water birds, coots without number, water hens, dab-chicks and ducks of many kinds (mallard, widgeon, teal, tufted duck). When there is a wind the water becomes choppy, and all these birds take shelter in the calmer waters of the great reed beds, and become invisible. In October there were a number of little stints, resembling snipe, but much smaller.

They were on the margin, just along where a certain rare plant grows. These birds come from the northern coasts of Siberia, and are so little afraid of mankind that you can nearly take them in the hand.

In another year, as early as 22 September, we witnessed a great outward migration of swallows. For a whole hour near sunset a broad stream of swallows was passing out over the ley and crossing the sea about in line with Start Point. Then as it got dark the great stream of birds stopped crossing the water, and formed into a great cloud over the ley. They poured down into the reeds, which were weighed down with them. Some individual reeds had each half a dozen swallows all twittering loudly. I looked again just as the sun rose next morning, but they were all gone. We paid many visits to this attractive bird resort.

In December 1895 I had been called upon to bring home my sister Eleanor for Christmas from St. Malo. The little boat took 15 hours to get across in the teeth of a gale. When the hatch was opened the sea came down to the cabin and broke up the crockery and flooded the place. Before returning we went to Mont St. Michel to see the beautiful Abbey, the monastery, and the dungeons below, which had models of rats biting men's toes. Then Madame Poulard roasted a small chicken for us, and boasted that she could roast 36 at the same time, that is on long revolving rods in front of a wall of fire. Coming across on the return journey the boat deck was loaded with crates of mistletoe. The French people asked if we ate it!

In March 1896 at age 18½ I was suddenly called upon to accompany my father to Locarno on the Lago Maggiore, Northern Italy, where his sister was unwell. I had collected butterflies, and after breakfast on the first morning a beautiful Apollo butterfly settled right at my feet in the sunshine on the doorstep. Some of the rocks were decorated with blue Hepatica in flower. There were a lot of crocus in flower, acres of mauve and acres of white on the flat meadows by the River

2

Ticino. My father took me up through St. Gothard to Andermat and to the Urseren Tal above the tunnel. The grey wagtails in the stream were just like those on Devon streams and in the pines above the village a blackbird was singing loudly in English. The snow was 6 feet deep. So we went to Lake Lucerne and the Rigi. On the Rigi top snow was up to the first-floor windows. But there were masses of oxlips down by the lake and on the 25th (Lady Day) we witnessed a procession on its knees to the Cathedral. Thence we went to Rheims and Amiens Cathedrals. There were two cross-channel paddle steamers, the "Foam" and the "Wave". On the return journey the engines primed and we lay to in the trough of the sea and discovered how heavily such a boat could roll.

In Dartington we had a habit of seeing the sunrise from some high point as near mid-summer as the holidays allowed. On 16 June 1896 I went alone from Dartington on a push-bike at midnight, being keen to see the sunrise from Rippon Tor on Dartmoor. Having hidden the bicycle and starting to walk up the Tor, I witnessed a wonderful performance, a Black Cock dance. The cocks spread their curved tails widely. Their wings having some white feathers, and they literally danced around a hen bird bowing to it. I watched this display for a few minutes. But if I was to be at the top in time for sunrise I had to interrupt it. The sunrise was truly beautiful. I longed to help others to see it, so I tried to paint, but I soon realized the impossibility. The skylarks and pipits were singing that beautiful morning. I knew of a snipe's nest in the marsh below and tried to snap a photo of the bird leaving the nest but of course the shutter was not nearly fast enough.

Soon after this I went to a tutor for a few weeks at Ilfracombe, staying with my Uncle Richard Martin at the Vicarage. There, one Sunday, I came out of the church after mattins while he remained for a second Communion Service. I saw boys tickling trout on the stream in the garden. I stalked them and took their basket with one trout. After lunch three boys were outside the door. I heard one say, "He's a kind old man, ask him." The basket belonged to a local fishmonger, and was wanted for Monday morning. He did ask and got the basket back, without the trout, but with a word of fatherly advice.

There were a lot of foxes in Dartington in the nineties. We sometimes lay awake at midnight and listened to them "wailing to the moon" as we called it. This was on warm moonlight nights. But in 1896 I was the only son at home, and had to go out much alone. One or two days a week I got up at first dawn if it was fine, "as soon as I could see the blackbirds on the lawn." And I went out with field-glasses and a gun as the rabbits were a plague. I sometimes brought in half a dozen and got 10d. each for them in Totnes. One morning after my first prowl around through the wood, mostly watching birds, I happened to see fox cubs at play. This was in a warm sunny corner of the top orchard. They tumbled over one another in their play, just like kittens, the mother fox looking on and admiring them. They were happy. That summer there was an old dog fox which seemed to be a bit blind. He nearly ran into me one morning.

Speaking of foxes if I may anticipate a little, at my first tutorship, by the River Aubeg in Southern Ireland, a fox had his earth in steep rocks across the river, right opposite our windows. And when the hounds had been out a good while a fox would come home into the wood, and sit quietly on top of the little cliff. When the hounds entered the wood, he walked quietly down to his earth on the cliff and the hounds had to be called off. Three years later again at my first curacy at Beeston, a parish of 12,000 population, one fine Monday morning in spring I received a telegram (to the surprise of the Post Office) from the wife of Bishop Ridding who ordained me, bidding me to come over and birds nest at Thurgaton Priory. My Vicar agreed. We saw some nice nests that day. But coming out of a wood on to a pasture, a fox ran across in front of us with a farm cockerel slung on his back. On the spur of the moment I threw a walking stick by

the tip. It spun and hit the fox across the neck. He dropped
the dead fowl and had to face a good scolding from the vixen
and the cubs.

When I was in the Botany School at Oxford my vacations
were spent at Dartington and I naturally did a lot of botanizing, especially collecting Mosses. In those days Mr. Twyford
was in charge of the woods for my cousin Arthur Champernowne. I spent most time in the glebe woods, but went also
more sparingly to those of my cousin. I have 70 years later
had a letter from a daughter of Mr. Twyford. She was very
young in the nineties, but she remembers her father coming
home and saying "that young Martin has been collecting
specimens just where I was trying to get the pheasants to lay,"
or something to that effect.

I tried to illustrate the mosses by mere shadows from a
candle 15 feet away on a half size photographic plate, with enlarged models of the fruits. The shadows were so perfect that
even the cells of the leaf could be sometimes seen with the
magnifying glass. I was still collecting butterflies, and moths,
a pursuit which was followed for 15 years. In the summer
evenings we had in those years many visits from the large
Convolvulus hawk moths dipping their tongues into the
geranium flowers under the windows and "Large Elephant"
hawk moths came to the French honeysuckle on the house,
sometimes two or three at a time; and many interesting
noctuae came to light in the porch room, especially about
11 p.m.

On two different occasions we saw the danger of cliff
climbing with a rope, and in general we would say "Don't
do it". "You really need a fencing mask" was the remark of
Amyas Champernowne who was with me. This was probably
in the spring of 1896. We were on the chalk cliff of Ballard
Point near Swanage, and the rope released flints from the
cliff edge. There were some cormorants' nests with eggs,
nests made of a quantity of seaweed smelling high. But there
was also a peregrine falcon's nest with young birds. They

like a high cliff or a cathedral spire. This one was specially interesting, because botanizing on Studland Heath not far away we came across the feathers of a carrier pigeon. Where it fell, there were two breast feathers of the peregrine (a falcon strikes the head of its prey in flight and death is instantaneous) and a few yards away was a little mound about a foot high. The pigeon had been carried to this and dismembered before feeding to the young. Two legs were left there, one bearing a ring with "J.G." and a number, and there were more breast feathers of the peregrine falcon. The ring was duly sent to a Homing Pigeon Society but the owner was not found.

On the approach to Studland Heath at that time was a fine show of large gorse bushes in full flower, and we saw several Dartford warblers (sometimes called furze wrens), with reddish breast and long tails, more than one cock bird at a time flitting up from the gorse flowers in song, after the manner of the whitethroat. We did not disturb them. Finding the nest would be a prickly job in such dense gorse. Amyas remarked that the man who first found the nest ought to have had a Victoria Cross (this was in the reign of Queen Victoria). Unfortunately the burning of gorse has since made the Dartford warblers very rare in this country.

* A WALK ON DARTMOOR

In late September 1898, three boys lost their way on the top of Dartmoor, where the ling was still in flower and the bilberry in fruit.

I was with my youngest brother that night and Hubert Brossault, the son of a Bordeaux wine merchant who was

staying with us at Dartington to improve his English. I was
the oldest of the three and responsible for the walk. It is hard
to believe that three boys aged 17–21 should have failed to
realize that we had turned into the wind. We were very
hungry: we had eaten our small sandwiches at Cranmere
Pool after walking from Postbridge, while we were waiting
for the artillery fire to stop. We then walked on to Yes Tor
in the late afternoon and back down the west side of the moor
under Amicombe Hill. Meanwhile a storm was blowing up,
the mist and darkness closed in on us with drenching rain.
There, in darkness, driving rain and dense mist, we tried to
consult a compass with the help of fusee matches, but this
was a total failure. (Electric torches had not been invented.)
We were on the south-west slope of Cut Hill and intended
to walk to the East Dart, but instead went to Cut Hill brook,
a small tributary of the Tavy, an error of about a right angle.
We then followed the stream. We could hear it if we could
not see it. But for several miles none of us perceived that we
were coming round to face the wind instead of having it
behind our backs. It was inexperience. When in the clouds
on moors or mountains keep the wind on the correct cheek.
After walking in a circle round Fur Tor we were on the
north side of Tavy Cleave, and when we came to the steep
part in the darkness we had to stop, Hubert Brossault was
tired and wanted to sleep *Qui dors dine*. "Who sleeps dines"
he said. There was plenty of bracken so I covered him with
a good heap and he apparently slept.

At one o'clock the moon rose and the mist lifted a little.
We could see the swollen torrent and—not without some
anxiety I saw my youngest brother holding to a boulder with
the torrent up to his waist—we got through it to the less
steep south side. We ate a few red blackberries and walked
on seven miles down to Tavistock by 7 o'clock, and eventually
got into the Newmarket Hotel by throwing small pebbles
into the open bedroom window of the proprietor. They did
us well, with good fire and bathroom and excellent breakfast,

and so back by train to Princetown and walking to Postbridge. There were no mutual recriminations and we never
heard what Monsieur Brossault, Hubert's father, said about
us. He had entrusted his son to us, and we got him lost on
the moor on a stormy night, but he doubtless expressed himself in French, and that would not have troubled our understanding much at that period.

Another walk somewhere about this period was from
Plymouth to Buckfastleigh across the southern half of Dartmoor. This was with Frank Champernowne, a most enter-
prising spirit, and Admiral Bradford, who had been my
uncle's second in command on the old H.M.S. *Mutine* of 1885
on the China Station. We walked via Kratta Barrow, but the
weather proved very wet. And we were so drenched by the
time we got to the River Avon, that Frank Champernowne
said he could get no wetter and walked through the peaty
flood. We followed, jumping with difficulty from one boulder
to another. We were, however, so wet when we got to
Buckfastleigh that, entering a small hotel, Bradford ordered
whisky and poured some of it into his boots to warm his feet,
asserting that Irish people always did so. We thought they
had somewhere else to put it!

Frank Champernowne was a cousin for whom we had a
youthful admiration, another great nephew of John Keble.
We believe that when his father Richard Champernowne was
Rector of Dartington, Frank had an unfortunate accident:
when he got over the fence from Parsonage Copse to enter
Brock's Park Copse, with his gun loaded, it went off, and he
lost his right hand. But he afterwards so trained his left hand
that he painted flowers very beautifully on wood panels and
cupboard doors. He played a fairly good game of tennis with
his left hand, balancing the ball on the racquet to serve. He
was a gay spirit. He later held some office at Keble College,
Oxford (Treasurer I think). Several years later (1911) we
met Frank Champernowne at Keble College. I had taken my
wife to see Oxford with my son who was a few months old.

We stayed in King Edward Street. We had no cot, so the small child slept in a drawer.

The ground we had crossed in the walk mentioned above included the area where we later had inexpensive holidays from 1904–14 in camp.

✳ AT COLLEGE

My father had lectured on Greek Philosophy at Christ Church in Oxford. I was to go to Christ Church and he wanted me to take Greek Philosophy for my degree. This meant being at Dartington for a year (1895–96) between school and university in order to study under his tuition. Also I agreed with him that if I studied Aristotle and Plato, I should take it for a pass degree only, and take Botany as another subject. I remember little of Aristotle except his definition of *happiness* as *Energeia kat aristaion*, "Active work in accord with virtue" —which I have found very true. Good work is indeed the greatest happiness for us all.

In September 1896 I went to Christ Church, Oxford, known as "The House" (Aedes Christi), and entering rooms near Canterbury Gate a tall scout named Ringrose greeted me on arrival, saying: "I am proud to show you into the very rooms occupied by Mr. Gladstone." The next day the freshman walked into the rooms of his tutor, C. M. Blagden. I was his first undergraduate pupil. And he told me later on that he had been very nervous of this first tutorial interview. But the newcomer was not a very terrifying person, and although I was a keen naturalist, I was determined to study enough to take my degree, and we got on very well together.

While I was up Mr. Blagden was ordained and he was later Bishop of Peterborough.

The Dean (Francis Paget, afterwards Bishop of Oxford) was very good to us all, giving an open invitation to House men to come to tea on Sunday afternoons. And we availed ourselves of it. He was very clever at talking to each on his individual interests. Mrs. Paget (*née* Helen Church) was also good at it. Her sister Mary Church was sometimes there also. They were daughters of the Dean of St. Paul's. Miss Church told me one day that she found it difficult to sleep in the early mornings at the Deanery in Oxford because of the "noise" the birds made! She had not noticed the incessant horse traffic near St. Paul's in London. Previous to my coming up, the Dean had put a stop to undergraduates attending the Blenheim ball as it involved being out for half the night, and some undergraduates had shown much ill will in consequence, but this had soon passed, and the Dean had become very popular. So much so that in the spring of 1897, when one young man wrote an unkind letter about the Dean in the *Oxford Magazine*, he received a note that he was to be in boating shorts by 6 p.m. as he was to be dipped in "Mercury", the fountain fish pool in Tom Quad. This was duly accomplished and he ran dripping past me into Peckwater Quad. We were usually orderly and it was beneath our dignity to walk the streets without wearing gown, and we did not smoke in public. Old Professor Dodgson had retired but we often saw him in and out of the College. As "Lewis Carroll" he had written *Alice in Wonderland*. Alice was a previous Dean's daughter. We were told that Queen Victoria was so pleased with *Alice* that she asked him to send his next book, which he did. It was on *Differential Calculus*. He was a mathematics professor.

It must have been early summer of 1897 that Edward Prince of Wales and Alexandra came to Oxford. The Prince was to open the new City Town Hall, a short distance above Tom Gate in St. Aldates. The Prince and Princess were staying at the Deanery, and they dined with us in Hall that

evening. And after dinner, it being still daylight, we were
allowed to take the horses out of his carriage and to pull the
carriage out through Tom Gate and up St. Aldates to the
Town Hall, where the Prince just waved his hand for us to
stop. But a number of Metropolitan Police had been brought
to Oxford for the occasion. Probably they had been a bit
annoyed already by an Oxford crowd. Anyhow they collared
many of us, as we were within the enclosure that was cor-
doned off. Some fought the police and were thrown on the
ground. So the several police cells under the Town Hall were
all filled with undergraduates the first night. I belonged to a
group which always respected law and order, and we got
back through Tom Gate before closing time, but the fight,
which the London police had really started through mis-
understanding, turned into a town and gown row, and rioting
went on till at least 11 o'clock. At that time I was sitting at
my window in Canterbury Quad with friends, looking out
along King Edward Street, and we saw mounted police turn
towards us from High Street, dispersing the crowds with
batons. And I always said that there was a rifle match the
next day, and one of the team had to be got out of imprison-
ment. At a later date Prince George, then Duke of York, and
Princess Mary also came to Christ Church and dined in Hall.
The next morning we had a parade of the Volunteer Corps in
Tom Quad and he inspected us. We well remember him.

I was a keen member of the Volunteers, much occupied
with rifle practice. And it must have been only a few weeks
after the above incident that the whole Oxford company went
into camp at Hyde Park on the occasion of Queen Victoria's
Diamond Jubilee. At dawn (4 a.m.) I took some companions
to bathe in the Serpentine. The water was dirty and I did not
see that the edge was very shallow. Taking a header I skinned
both knees on the gravel bottom. So I had to stand all day
with handkerchiefs tied round both of them. The breakfast
ran grievously short. We always said that only three whole
cheeses and no bread came to our battalion. (That morning

the yellow hammers must have changed their tune and sung
"Little bit of cheese and no bread".) I think we all had
biscuits and brandy in our haversacks. We were posted near
St. Thomas's Hospital across an opening in buildings south
of Westminster Bridge, 8 a.m. to 4 p.m. I was a corporal
and we not unexpectedly had to help some who fainted with
hunger, especially as we had hot sun on our backs. This was
all in the day's work for a humble young man blessed with
a healthy body. But we duly saluted Queen Victoria. I remember her well. Her carriage was preceded by Captain Amery,
the tallest man in the British Army, on an outsize horse. We
had a good meal after 4 p.m.

Like most others I went pretty regularly in my first year
to the College barge for training in rowing, but I was of too
light a weight. I did train for Torpids as a bow oar or spare
man. For this we ran round the meadow every morning
before having breakfast together, which included eating a
half-raw chop. This was very different from my normal breakfast. I was a great expense to my father, and I tried to keep
down the College battels or bills. So for nearly three years
my breakfast consisted of a bowl of porridge from the College
kitchen at a penny, an egg from the creamery at Carfax also
a penny, with bread and butter, etc. As I was not wanted in
an eight, I took to sculling like others, mostly on the upper
river, and entered for a sculling race at the end of the Summer
Term, when the weed in the river was very heavy. I was, I
thought, getting on well, but my scull caught in the weed
opposite a crowded university boat-house, and of course the
water closed over my head, to their amusement. A skiff or a
whiff is mainly balanced by the sculls on the water.

We were a happy group in Meadow Buildings. The
Cathedral was our College Chapel and we attended the Holy
Communion regularly on Sundays and also College Prayers
daily before breakfast. This last was indeed an item in the
rules and those who missed it on several days were sum-
moned before the Senior Censor to explain their absence. The

Senior Censor was Tommy Strong, who also afterwards became Dean of Christ Church and later Bishop of Ripon. My maternal Uncle Walter Moberly was Professor of Pastoral Theology. He lived next to the Cathedral, and I was rather frequently in his house. But it is surprising to me now that I was never called upon to attend his lectures or those of Canon Inge, Professor of Divinity, or of Dr. Bright, the authority on early church history. I listened to their sermons which taught me quite a bit. Dr. Bright in the most impressive passage of his sermon used to look at us over his spectacles, leaning his arms over the pulpit cushion. But, as mentioned above, I was taking Greek Philosophy and Botany with Church History.

So I landed at the Botanic Garden under Professor Vines. He was assisted by Mr. A. W. Church who impressed upon students the necessity of drawing any decent specimen that they saw under the microscope. I had to start making drawings, poor things they were. The lectures covered all aspects of plant life. I was specially interested in the Mosses. I tried to figure the Mosses with enlargements of fruits and leaves, and set up many larger Mosses on cards which have sometimes been exhibited. But I started drawing flowers because fellow students complained of the difficulty of identifying them from the long wordy descriptions in works then available.

At the end of the century I was always hunting for Mosses in fruit, and there was one which intrigued me. I had often seen it on Dartmoor but not in fruit. It was called *Breutelia arcuata*, which seems to be rarely in fruit. And all of a sudden I found it on the steep slope above the River Exe on Exmoor. I was so absorbed that I didn't see the approach of a stag, and the stag didn't see me. He had come out of the bracken further up and had come down to the river for a drink before grazing at sunset. A fine old stag. I had crossed the little stream of the head of the Exe 20 yards further up, and in consequence the stream carried the scent of me down to the stag who was drinking. Suddenly he got scent of me and he looked up sharply. I looked up at the same moment, and there we were, face to face. Immediately the stag began bouncing up the very steep slope on the other side. There was a little projecting rock and he stood with his four feet together. There was just room for his four feet, a lovely picture. And he had a good stare at me. And then he decided that I was dangerous and he went off up the hill and along the top, with antlers laid on his back. I had no rifle, but he didn't know that.

But I was also interested in other aspects of natural history both at Dartington and at Oxford, where during my three years I walked almost daily round Christ Church meadow before lectures. Round the meadow there were not only flowers but birds, including all the year round a compact colony of tree sparrows with conspicuous black blotch on a white cheek. These were always in old willows by the River Cherwell. The nuthatches in the Broad Walk were fed daily with nuts on my balcony at the top of No. 1 Meadow Buildings. The nuts were fixed under irons so that they had to be cracked in front of the window. If a nut slipped out the bird dived down and caught it in his beak and carried it to an old elm, fixing it in a crevice in the bark for cracking.

We used bicycles continually. They were not allowed in college. They were kept at a shop in the town, where necessary repairs, punctures and brake adjustments were seen to very ably by a young man named Morris, later Lord Nuffield.

Bicycles took us to various beauty spots including Bablock Hythe on the river a few miles west of Oxford. It was there one day that I looked too closely at a whitethroat's nest, and the mother bird slipped off the nest amongst the brambles, and struggled on her side along the ground, pretending to have a broken wing, in order to draw the intruder from the nest. At Oxford I made the acquaintance of Mr. Druce, the chemist, afterwards Dr. Druce, a famous botanist and Fellow of the Royal Society. In later years he sent me many rare local flowers from all parts of the British Isles. These sound like individual activities, but we had plenty of social life. We had good friends.

We attended lectures together and wore our gowns for dining in Hall together. We met for tea or more often for coffee parties in one another's rooms, about 10 p.m. A pound of pipe tobacco cost very little in those days. A party of us went together to the Christ Church Mission in Poplar, East London, to do an easy item of visiting, looking up Sunday scholars.

I shall always remember the final Examination before taking my degree. We each sat at a little table which was provided with a large inkpot, and two quill pens in the old style. And my viva voce exam. was taken by Dr. Spooner. We were always looking out for "Spoonerisms" in his talk.

At Oxford I was in the University Rifle Eight, and as Secretary of the "Shooting Committee" helped to organize practices at the local Hincksey Range. And I was troublesome to those who would not practice, calling upon men in other Colleges to go to the range for practice. "If they were to be in the Volunteers they must be efficient rifle shots." I naturally helped in the training. And the standard of marksmanship certainly improved, so that in 1899 Cambridge was soundly beaten at Bisley for the first time for several years. We usually went to Bisley for the whole week in order to get practice there before the match, and we were about able to earn enough in money prizes to pay our way. The Hincksey range at Oxford was however closed owing to the introduction of the more penetrating Lee Metford rifle. So the team and other volunteers went several times to the range at Witney. This was not far and was a favourite. The range was closely bordered by beautiful woodlands, filled in early summer with bluebells and the songs of familiar woodland birds, including nightingales. I appreciated this. I was recording bird migration at the time. Sometimes we went to the Reading range, where we met the Winchester boys. Sometimes we arranged for the team to go to other schools including Clifton and Rugby for a match on their range. We went into barracks at Aldershot where I had to lead an example of kneeling for prayers—32 in a room. And I was hare in a paper chase. We were in barracks with some Gordon Highlanders at the time, and some of these joined in the paper chase in kilties. I unfortunately led them through a gorse common. So their knees were much scratched. (A few years later again as a hare in my time at Cuddesdon I led my fellow students as hounds through some gorse on Horsepath Hill.)

In Volunteers we had helped to train a good many in rifle practice. We little knew what was coming. Soon after I took my degree the South African war began. And in early days it was going badly for the British Forces. I always said that a young officer with the Army in South Africa wrote home to the papers saying "Are all the gentlemen of England foxhunting?" and that partly as a result of this, Oxford sent a whole company of university men in the local Oxfordshire Volunteer battalion, and that the name of the officer who wrote to the paper was Winston Churchill. Most of my friends were therefore going to South Africa. I was going, but I had for a long while been intending to be ordained, and my father held the view that I must give up one or the other. He insisted that if I went to the war I must promise him that I would not be ordained to the Ministry of the Church, because the two aims were quite inconsistent. David was not allowed to build the temple because he had shed blood. I was reduced to sending a telegram to say that I could not sail with them, and felt something of a deserter.

But perhaps the Volunteer training was of some use (I found myself a few years later Chaplain of the Royal North Lancashire Regiment at Lancaster and later still a Chaplain to forces in France in the First World War).

The South African war, however, was an unfortunate business. It was two white races fighting in the presence of the black. And it embittered the relations of British and Dutch in a manner difficult to overcome. The British won in the fighting and then lost it by diplomacy because soon afterwards (1906) Britain generously made the colony into a self-governing Dominion in which the Dutch people had a majority. And they promptly dismissed a large number of the British Civil Servants under the Colonial Office. This included some of my special friends. One of them, Oscar Watkins, was given a post as District Commissioner in East Africa.

Galanthus nivalis (Snowdrops)

* AS A TUTOR 1899-1901

At the end of 1899 the first drawing for the *Concise British Flora* was made at Dartington; snowdrops against ivy leaves, the first and last made against leaves not related to the flower.

Waiting for a place at Cuddesdon Theology College, I had to go and earn my living, so there follow three little pictures of life as a tutor. First at Castletownroche in Southern Ireland, landing at Waterford, the train to Co. Cork (Sept. 1899) was collecting young men called up for service in South Africa on their way to training at Fermoy, and there was much weeping on the platforms. That autumn the weather was mild and the women seemed to be doing the work in the fields, lifting potatoes. Were their husbands doing the housework? Sometimes on Sundays we saw men with huge pockets full of game from the landlord's woods. The little English Church was dull and poorly supported. We drove to Fermoy, for shopping, in a side-car with a good horse, our legs out over the wheels. At a cottage below the road a big pig was apt to be rubbing himself against a cottage door-post. He gave chase hoping for scraps and kept up with the horse. South of the house where I was working the park was bordered by a wooded slope down to the little River Aubeg. From October this bit of scrub and wood was full of woodcock which flew out at dusk with their long beaks pointing downwards; they went to feed in wet meadows below. The Nagles Moors were much like our native Dartmoor, having the same moorland plants. Around the house there was a quantity

Geranium robertianum (Herb Robert)

of Herb Robert geranium. This and the enlargement of Stitchwort were the second and third items drawn for the *Concise British Flora*.

Next for two terms I was filling a gap in the staff of a private boys' school at Malvern. The summer term and the games field were of chief interest. Teaching boys to hold a cricket bat upright or showing them a few birds' nests. A butcher bird made his nest and larder in the hedge of the cricket field. And the long grass of the railway embankment harboured no less than six whinchats' nests, which you discover by walking backwards, because they visit the closely hidden nest after you have passed. I saw a cuckoo carry an egg to a wheatear's nest which I had just found in a rabbit hole on the Malvern Hills. I was longing to teach about the flowers and I drew for the boys' instruction a big plate of enlarged Rose flowers in section, but it was not used in the *Concise British Flora*. We attended the Abbey Church.

In Malvern I needed a dentist. He had a long beard which got in his way. But he was interesting. He told me that skeletons of Etruscans had been found, with teeth nicely stopped. They were buried centuries before Rome was founded.

Cockbaria danica
(Scurvey-grass)

Then I became a family tutor, with one pupil preparing for matriculation and a younger brother. This at first was at Henley-on-Thames, where the tutor had to live in a lodging, and only came in for school hours, an amazingly lonely arrangement. The tutor was a member of the British Ornithologists' Union and keen on bird protection, and the first evening he was invited in to dinner, we sat down to lark pie, of all things, with legs sticking out through the pastry! It was special and for his welcome. He was a new arrival and on his best behaviour! (Sept. 1900).

The next term I lived in; this was at Brighton, and one drawing of a common little Scurvy-grass took its place on a plate. Then we had a summer term at Yarner, near Bovey Tracey, where the house was at the head of a square mile of woodland on the steep slopes of Dartmoor. The top fence just above the house divided the woodland birds from those of the moor, the warblers from the chats, the tree pipits from meadow pipits. Greater spotted woodpeckers brought up a family in a poplar within a few feet of my bedroom window. We played tennis until the nightjars came out catching moths. I happened to find the strong new locality for the rare plant *Lobelia urens*. Kew herbarium and the Natural History Museum were supplied with specimens. I drew it and recorded it in the *Journal of Botany*, 1901, *p.* 428. I well remember on fine Sunday mornings bicycling down to Bovey Tracey Church and pushing the bike up again 1,100 feet before breakfast.

Lobelia urens

* AT CUDDESDON THEOLOGICAL COLLEGE 1901-2
A Happy Life, a Small Fire and a Big Expedition

In September 1901 I went to Cuddesdon and was there until December 1902 except for vacations. At first I was in a room on the top floor of the old building. We each had a small bedroom behind a wooden partition. It was indeed a very happy time. The unity of purpose and spirit in the service of our Lord produced a brotherly kindness and co-operation which was most felicitous and soon dissolved any doubts that had arisen through natural science studies and Darwin's ideas of evolution. After all, evolution appears to be just the Divine method of Creation. "The Mills of God grind slowly."

I had studied Botany for my degree and had read a good deal of Darwin's *Origin of Species* and the Duke of Argyle's definition of Natural Law so called. Nature to me was beautiful. And beauty of anything seems to come only from personality. Not only does evolution seem to be the Divine method of making things beautiful. But Natural Law is only "part of the consistent regularity of the method by which God continuously wills that the universe should be sustained and developed". The method includes other aspects which transcend the regularity just as in human personality, and these aspects appear to us as miraculous, so "consider the birds" (and their songs). "Consider the lilies", because so far as we know it is only personality that can make or appreciate beauty.

The curriculum at Cuddesdon included a full round of daily services and lectures. Prime, Holy Communion, lectures, Sext, and finishing with Compline at night.

We often attended a mattins or evensong in the Parish

Church close by, wearing open surplices. One day coming back from church still surpliced, I found the top floor full of smoke. It was spurting out at the edges of the door next to mine ("Mother" Earle's room. Earle was a dear good man. I had been his "fag" at Marlborough). I fetched a jug of water quickly from my room, burst the door open and emptied the jug on a big blaze in the middle of the room, and shouting for help emptied all the jugs from top floor rooms before help came. A large basket arm-chair in front of a coal fire had been entirely burnt and other furniture all alight, a big hole in the floor, and the varnish on the wooden partition blistered and ready to catch alight. It was a near enough escape for the old building. It was end of term. Like many others I moved later to rooms outside, where my window looked out on to Bishop Paget's kitchen garden and a pair of lesser spotted wood-peckers nested conveniently in an old apple-tree opposite my window.

In the afternoons we had good walks or played Association Football, and had some matches. We had one paper chase in which I was a hare and laid some false trails for them over Shotover Hill way.

✷ 1902

I believe the Summer Term (1902) ended rather early about 9 July, and I arranged a walk with a friend in order to see the sunrise on the Brecon Beacons and collect flowers there, before going back to Dartington. My walking companion failed to turn up, so I was alone at the Castle Inn, Brecon. Sunday was a very hot day and I attended all the services at the Parish Church, the heavy stonework of which made it the one cool place. Taking a short rest after evensong I was called at 11 p.m. for a light meal. In the hotel was a Colonel in command of a Devonshire battalion in camp under Brecon

Beacons. He, good kindly man, fortunately marked on my inch ordnance map the position of the camp, which was under a wood in Cwm Llwch. I set off before midnight on the ten or eleven miles up Afon Tarell, not by the main road but by a small track with the stream below me on the right. There was low scrub or bushes by the stream. At first the silence was impressive. But soon came a section where there were grasshopper warblers in the low scrub by the stream, singing lustily in the summer twilight. The song is curious and like the sound of a fisherman's reel running out. They seem very local and in really wild growth. Then following the Glyn Tarell stream to its source, and some two miles eastward on to the open moor, I hurried for fear of being late for sunrise, and lost a pair of field-glasses from the pocket of my jacket, which I was carrying because it was so warm. I arrived at the top of the cliff edge ten minutes before the sun appeared. And when it came, how glorious it was! The north face of Pen-y-fan is an irregular precipitous cliff about a mile long. There were beautiful cloud ripples about 1,000 feet below me, and the sun lighted the top of those ripples first with crimson then with golden light. Some thanksgiving for it was inevitable. Just near me at the top the mossy Saxifrage was a mass of flower like a white tablecloth. I chose some little bits for drawing. Then I heard a voice calling me. Where could it come from on that lonely top at 4 a.m.? Some precipitous cliffs there almost face one another. There were two young men on a ledge below, with a 40-foot straight wall above them. This was Monday and they had climbed up on Sunday morning, and one of them was sick and giddy, and his friend had stayed with him all day and all night. They were starving and first I tried to do the wrong thing. I tried to toss them bits of my breakfast; most dangerous for them reaching out in vain to catch it. Then I called out to them: "Stay patiently where you are and I will get plenty of help." I ran down 2,000 feet (how my hips ached after it!) to the camp in Cwm Llwch. The Commandant sent a squad of men,

two mules laden with stout ropes, the camp doctor, some food
and a stone ginger beer bottle half-full of fairly strong brandy.
I led the way. Loops were made in the rope to go under the
sick man's arms, after his "ginger beer". He was pulled to
the top, right across the mossy Saxifrage, but stones the size
of brick-bats flew past his head. It was a dangerous proceeding. He was landed on top just at 12 noon. His friend climbed
down and eventually joined us. They had been more than
24 hours on the cliff. We learned that they were clerks in a
colliery office at Merthyr Tydfil but did not learn their names.
They certainly missed their Monday in the office. We still
have the map on which the colonel marked the camp and a
rifle range. It was a beautiful and
useful sunrise walk. The beauty and
silence of which was suddenly
changed to effort.

But sunrise walks are not always a
success. Some years later I persuaded
my two eldest sisters to go with me
to see the sunrise from Cawsand
Beacon at the north-east corner of
Dartmoor. We had a nice walk to the
top but it was cloudy. A little slit in
the cloud, like a half-open eye,
enabled us to get a small glimpse of
the sun. Then the rain came down,
and we were well drenched.

Saxifraga hypnoides
(Mossy Saxifrage)

In the Autumn Term at Cuddesdon (1902) I was preparing in earnest for my life's work. The Principal, J. O. Johnston, was a great help to me both in his addresses and his private advice. The time had come for choosing a suitable sphere of work. I had lived among the woods and moors of Devon, and was quite keen to work hard in some big industrial parish, and asked for this. The Vicar of Beeston, Notts., a parish of 12,000, came to Cuddesdon looking for an assistant curate; and I was immediately booked for this. I was ordained deacon on St. Thomas's Day, 21 December, by the Bishop of Southwell, George Ridding, in Southwell Minster, and ordained priest a year later.

✷ BEESTON

George Ridding was a good bishop, and a good adviser. He drew up an excellent Litany for use by the clergy, and it was used at all meetings of clergy in the diocese. He had to make Derby and Notts. into a diocese. He had been Headmaster at Winchester and his first wife was my mother's sister. Like many others she died in childbirth. His second wife was a sister of the Earl of Selborne. She insisted on our calling her "Aunt" Lolly. She was a very able bishop's wife, and was on all sorts of diocesan committees. She looked after such small fry as ordination candidates very well. She was a bit masterful and saw that they were on the station, which was near by, at least 15 minutes before the train was due. She was very good to me. And I occasionally went over to Thurgaton Priory, where they lived, for a happy day in the country.✷

✷ I happened to be in the Bishop's study when his nephew, another George Ridding, was licensed to the curacy of East Retford. And oddly enough this nephew's son, a third George Ridding, when he was working as a School Chaplain in Exeter, more than 60 years later, has sometimes taken my place at the early Communion services at Exton in Woodbury, when I had to be away from home. He is now Head of the Cathedral School in Bombay.

So my main life's work began, when I was 25 years of age, in Christmas week 1902 in the large parish of Beeston, an industrial suburb of Nottingham. And I was at Beeston for nearly four years. Arthur Beckton was Vicar, dear good man. I had a fellow curate, John R. Lee, steady, serious and spectacled. I was to take the Valley Mission district, to do not less than 30 visits a week, to look after the sick people, to study quite a lot and to teach at the Valley Mission and its Sunday School. This was a big Sunday School with about 500 scholars and was opposite to the entrance of the Humber Works, which mostly made bicycles in those days. The Sunday School was under the able superintendence of Mr. Hayes. I most often took Sunday evensong and preached at this Mission, and sometimes went to supper afterwards with a lay reader, Mr. Elliott, and his wife, whose small daughter has written to remind me of it more than 60 years later. I was very happy in the work.

In winter it was apt to be densely foggy in that smoky Trent Valley. But on the first Sunday in September one year we had very hot weather. It happened that I had to hurry to the Parish Church to get a register before walking down to the Valley Mission Sunday School. There was a thermometer outside the vestry door in the shade and it registered the rare level of 95 degrees. I was wearing top hat and frock coat according to rule, not very suitable for such a temperature! And in the churchyard there were three or four large yellow lizards playing about. These had apparently come from big branches of bananas in an adjoining shop, the first bananas I ever saw. The lizards remained there for some weeks.

There was plenty of work to do at Beeston. In fact as the work had been neglected, there were whole families to be prepared for baptism. This fell to my lot. We assembled them usually round a kitchen table for a few lessons, insisting that all over 7 years of age attended. Some Sunday School teachers had to take part as godparents and large numbers were baptized.

Convallaria majalis
(Lily of the Valley)

In the first early summer we enjoyed a nice trip with some of the young men, who were Sunday School teachers. This was a long bicycle ride into the Derbyshire Peak district and the Via Gellia, where we saw children with arms full of Lilies of the Valley. We gathered a few in the woods, and one was duly drawn. The next autumn a bicycle ride to Nanpanton in the Charnwood Forest added Ciliated Pearlwort (Pl. 16).

We each had also our annual holiday in which we could visit our own people. My father was Rector of Dartington in South Devon. And he was wanting to visit his old haunts at Winchester. So on my first summer holiday (1903), I went with my father into rooms on Shawford Down near Winchester. We had a glimpse of Winchester College and of the Cathedral and St. Cross. The downs were of chalky soil and provided Kidney Vetch (Pl. 23) and the little Thesium (Pl. 75), also the Frog Orchis (Pl. 82). And then, in order to see more of the chalk plants, a trip was made with my brother Arthur, perhaps in the following year, to rooms at Beer in East Devon, where Rock Sea Lavender (*Limonium benervosum*) was added.

Thesium humifusum

Anthyllis vulneraria (Kidney Vetch)

Coeloglossum viride (Frog Orchis)

I had been very busy studying for my priest's exam, in addition to the sermons and class lessons, and I was ordained priest on St. Thomas's Day, 21 December 1903.

A form of recreation was the hiring of a boat on the River Trent. This provided a renewal of sculling exercise. It also took me across the river to Clifton Hall, where kind friends kept tame brown owls. They also had a tame monkey, which had a horrid habit at dinner time of sitting on the back of the chair of any visitor, and pretending to find extras in the hair of his head! In the Trent there was a fair amount of nice Water Buttercup (*Ranunculus trichophyllus*) (Pl. 2). This was

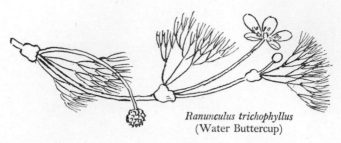

Ranunculus trichophyllus
(Water Buttercup)

the only place I ever met with this one. Two kinds of Burnet Saxifrage (*Pimpinella*) (Pl. 38) came from Sandy Lane at Beeston.

For a few months in 1904 the two assistant curates had rooms together in a house called "Cairnduna" and were looked after by our good verger, Mr. Rhodes, and his wife. This soon came to an end, however, with John Lee's departure. For in August 1904 Bishop Ridding died, and in due course Edwyn Hoskyns became Bishop of Southwell. And in February 1905, John Lee left Beeston to become Bishop's chaplain. So I was the only assistant curate. Amongst other things I started a boys' club in the other Sunday School in Brown Lane, with games and boxing and some gymnastics, and also a men's club at the Rylands on the Trent bank. There were chess players there, and I gave them two sets of chessmen. As a result an elderly Mrs. Robinson, who was interested in the Rylands, kindly gave me a beautiful set of vessels for sick Communion, which are still in use after 60 years.

In the early summer of 1905 a brief trip was made by train to Gainsborough and by bicycle to Scotton Common in Lincolnshire. This was made more for the birds than for the flowers. There in the marshes I was amongst a great quantity of duck of many varieties. I specially enjoyed watching the pretty little teal which was plentiful. But some interesting marsh plants were gathered, including Golden Dock (Pl. 74).

In July 1905 I also joined my brothers and a friend for a short and inexpensive camp on Dartmoor. We will refer to this later.

Pimpinella (Burnet Saxifrage)

Rumex maritimus (Golden Dock)

My vicar, Arthur Beckton, was a good preacher and much sought after. And on Sunday morning, 1 October 1905, he was preaching at a church in Nottingham, and after the service he had a very severe stroke. He was only 42. The stroke was made more severe, we believe, by an accident in earlier years. So on that Sunday I went quickly to the railway station in order to go and take his place at a church, where he was to preach in the afternoon. But it was 1 October. The train was taken off that very day and the station was being forcibly closed against several intending passengers. I bicycled. From that Sunday the good Vicar never spoke again. He could not sign his resignation and so remained officially Vicar. And I was alone for all the work, until the Bishop sent Cecil Saunders as curate-in-charge. Saunders, good man, had lately been an army chaplain in the South African War. He was fairly tall, and added to his dignity by looking at us through a single eye-glass. I stayed on with him for nearly a year, the visiting falling extensively to my lot, often fifty visits a week. Half the population was of a floating kind, as the place was suburban. I reckoned that there were about 600 new families as householders each year. And the Police Inspector agreed that it must be about this number.

My sister Eleanor shared my quarters with me for a short time, as she was teaching Mrs. Beckton's daughter. But for the most part of these years the lodgings seemed dull and lonely to come back to every day. There was no home companionship, or anyone to talk things over with at age 28 and 29. The curate admits that even in early Beeston days there was a strong attraction, for he was human. But this had seemed to interfere with his work, and had to be overcome (on his knees of course, why not say so, life is real). He never betrayed any sign of it. It was dismissed. The curate had no possessions except a minimum of clothing, and a writing-table, and just enough income to maintain himself alone. There was no possibility of getting married.

But that is not quite the end of the story. The lady belonged to a large family at a house which we will call "Willow Fields". And the family were very good to me, inviting me to tea and tennis in summer. And I tried to help two younger daughters a little in botany. My parents even invited a younger daughter to Dartington with her brother. They stayed there and came up and saw our camp on the moor. All unawares I had lost my heart to a younger daughter.

Meanwhile the Reverend Pitts Tucker was appointed Vicar of Beeston. I left and accepted a curacy at Ashbourne in Derbyshire. And six months or more after I had left, I bicycled about 25 miles to admit my tender feelings to the young lady's mother, as she was considerably under 21 years of age. But I had so far concealed my feelings, that the young lady had not guessed it, or thought of it. Her mother was rather severe about it. And the special circumstances seemed to make it necessary to break off contact. So ended this romance. I have no idea where these kind people moved to, but 60 years later I find that a member of my congregation at Exton was brought up from childhood, after my friends had left, in that very house, which we have called "Willow Fields" and which I used to frequent.

✳ ASHBOURNE, DERBYSHIRE

I arrived in Ashbourne in September 1906, and was lodged in a house kept by two sisters in Church Street near the Hall Hotel, that is at the far end from the church. The Vicar was Canon Morris, a dignified figure. He wore top hat and frock coat on all days. His assistant did so on Sundays only. The

Vicar had a family, and his eldest, a daughter, Evelyn, was
superintendent of the Sunday School. Evelyn Morris later
became a deaconess and gave her life to work for children
and old people in Bethlehem, and now at a great age she still
continues that work.

I attended the Parish Church daily and assisted at 8 a.m.
on Sundays, taking also a large proportion of the Sunday
services at the little daughter church at Mapleton near the
River Dove, and there was plenty of visiting to do although
there was a Church Army lady helping.

I also had a good deal of studying to do for my sermons,
as I believed in making them usefully instructive. I enjoyed
the visiting and was very happy at the services in the Parish
Church. For recreation I sometimes had rather lonely walks
to Ashbourne Green or Dove Dale after flowers. Occasionally
Dr. Hollick, the local practitioner, took me for a drive in his
dog-cart to any village he was visiting, or Frank Jourdain,*
an authority on birds, then Vicar of Clifton, took me out
bird watching on a Monday morning, and there was a mixed
Hockey Club in which I played occasionally down at May-
field. The Vicar kindly entertained the curate to luncheon on
Sundays.

The Parish Church was large and beautiful, with a high
spire. And the Vicar arranged for the verger (Mr. Haycock)
to ring a rousing bell at 7 o'clock on Sundays to help members
to get up for the 8 a.m. service. For some reason this was
sometimes omitted. The assistant curate was pretty keen,
and one Sunday he bicycled to the church before 7 a.m. to
ring this rousing bell. But when he entered the church, smoke
and sparks were spurting up through chinks in the floor
beside the organ. The heating chamber was below the organ,
and was evidently well stocked with fuel. He found that all
this high pile of fuel outside the stove was red hot and burning fiercely. He called up the verger quickly and they both

---

* Joint author of Kirkman and Jourdain's beautiful work on *British Birds*,
published in 1966.

spent the hour damping down the fuel fire, and shovelling it out on to the churchyard. Then dashing home to wash a black face and returning to help the Vicar in a smoky church.

Lodgings were rather lonely. The year 1907 provided plenty of work, but a lack of social life and companionship. There was no one of my own personal friends to talk things over with. My evening meal constantly included tartlets filled with lemon curd (I ate no lemon curd for years afterwards). I nearly always sat alone in the evening. This was a wonderful opportunity for study. But study does not seem to supply all our needs. One day I bicycled to Lincoln to see dear old Bishop Edward King, my father's friend, and had a nice talk with him as he sat in his purple cassock in spring sunshine. At that time the flat road from Newark to Lincoln was worn out and full of deep pot-holes. But either the trip or the Bishop cheered me very much.

✳ CAMPING HOLIDAYS

For these camps we took just a cart-load of tents, bedding and cooking materials from Dartington. The camp was on the Warren stream under Puppers Hill, in fact near the Warrener's cottage, about five miles west of Buckfastleigh. My brother Arthur kept a log-book or record of these camps, and the writer for his part made some early drawings of Purple Heather, Bilberry and Soft Rush.

Vaccinium myrtillus (Bilberry)

3

These camps on Dartmoor provided an inexpensive form of annual holiday at about midsummer, in several successive years, 1904–14, and each lasted for a week. We were six or eight young men together, mostly brothers and cousins, with a friend Walter Medlicott who was the soul of wit of the party, and his dog Buggins, and one year Dick Fellows from Beeston. I managed to get to the early camps, though I sometimes arrived a bit late as I could not leave Beeston until Monday morning, but had to miss 1910–13. They were all keen fishermen except the writer. I was hunting Mosses and bird watching. Each year we blocked the tumbling brook, the Warren stream, with rocks in order to make a bathing pool, into which we could take headers, i.e. dive in the early morning sunshine. The stream and the pool were full of trout. And after catching about a hundred, there were still nearly as many in the pool on the last day. We also had permission of the Duchy of Cornwall to shoot rabbits. We found it necessary to have bell tents, as these always presented the same kind of surface to the high winds, which often changed direction in the night. My brother Arthur was, like Medlicott, an architect, and he kept the camp log-book or record, and he made some beautiful drawings of the horse and cart that brought us, and of other critical moments. My brother Jack was another padre. We had a little sheltered gulley in the rocks, which was our church, and Arthur inscribed a cross at one end on an erect stone. We had our morning service here and called it Mattins Corner. (The Devonshire Association studied the cross 40 years later and decided that it was *not* medieval.) In the first year there was an infant in the Warrener's cottage whom we baptized for the Vicar of Lydford; the baptism had to be entered in the Church register 21 miles away as the crow flies. We had a Sunday evensong in the cottage also. I was once able to be present at it. This Warrener's cottage supplied us with milk and eggs, which was very convenient, and a postman came out there daily. Three Warrener's children walked daily five miles across the moor, sometimes in dense clouds, in order to attend school at Holne, carrying their luncheon with them. There were adders in the private corners of our camp, but we took no harm from them. The moorland adders have the spinal line and the "V" dark red instead of black. After I was married I still came. In 1914, just before the war began, the camp week was very warm. One day we slept in the afternoon and then went up to the moor top near Aune head and lay up at night. The dew was very heavy. In the midsummer midnight twilight we watched foxes hunting with dripping wet coats. The red grouse were calling warnings to their chicks, sounding like "Go back, go back, go back". Before sunrise the sky became filled with skylarks singing their prime; then they all came down and fed hurriedly on caterpillars, and as the sun broke the horizon, they all went up again and stayed up singing lustily. They were many and seemed utterly happy. Nature is very beautiful.

There was a young lady in her twenties living at Dove House in Ashbourne. She was an active, outdoor person. I saw her in Dove Dale. She was a member of the hockey team and a good tennis player. She was a very regular worshipper at the Parish Church, and I happened to discover that she played the piano beautifully (another valuable asset). The thought of her got lodged in my mind, till at the end of the year, I persuaded my good sister Dora to come on a visit to the Hall Hotel near by. And I ventured to invite Violet and her elder sister to tea in my room to meet Dora. After tea I told Dora my thoughts, which she had not guessed. Soon after this I proposed to Violet. It had been contrary to my principles to reveal attraction for ladies, and so I was met with the reply: "I do not even know you, Mr. Martin."

Violet had an elder sister in Ashbourne and also two brothers overseas. Her mother had died before I came to Ashbourne. Her father Henry Chaworth-Musters had a military moustache, and was said to be a bit erratic. He had been brought up in a big house, Colwick Hall, Nottingham. He was fond of horses and was commonly seen with whip and reins in hand, driving a high dog-cart. Those were the days of domestic servants. And a story told against him was that one day when he drove to Derby (13 miles) he was to bring back a new cook to Dove House. He put her on the back seat. On the back seat of a dog-cart we had to put an arm over the back of the seat to hold on by. Anyway he arrived at Ashbourne and the back seat was empty, and he had to go back and look for her.

Now I had proposed to this man's daughter. Long afterwards I was told that the family response was "The Curate has proposed to Violet: what cheek!" But as I knew by this time that I was on a list for early preferment, the idea was allowed to grow. And on 28 March 1908 we became engaged to be married. Violet's friends, the Gladwin-Erringtons of Hinchley Wood at Mapleton, were particularly kind and hospitable to the young couple.

My uncle, Richard Martin, at that time Vicar of Ilfracombe, North Devon, had several curates, and he made a rule that if one of his curates became engaged to a girl in the parish, he was always to leave and accept appointment elsewhere. I knew this. So, while waiting for a vicarage to turn up, I accepted the senior curacy of Lancaster Parish Church. I did not know what strenuous work I was in for there.

While I was working at Ashbourne only a few flowers were actually drawn. These included the Strawberry-headed Clova (*Trifolium fragiferum*), Pl. 23, and knotted Pearlwort (*Sagina nodosa*), Pl. 16. Both of these were from Ashbourne Green. Jacob's Ladder (*Polemonium caeruleum*), Pl. 5, was another. For this I reached down the steep bank of the Bentley Brook, my fiancée holding me by an ankle to prevent my falling (in 1908). A few others came from short visits to my parents at Dartington, including *Lotus tenuis* (Pl. 23) from the stiff clay of Newgrounds, and two common heathers (Pl. 55) from the camping holidays on Dartmoor, and *Juncus maritimus* from Dawlish Warren.

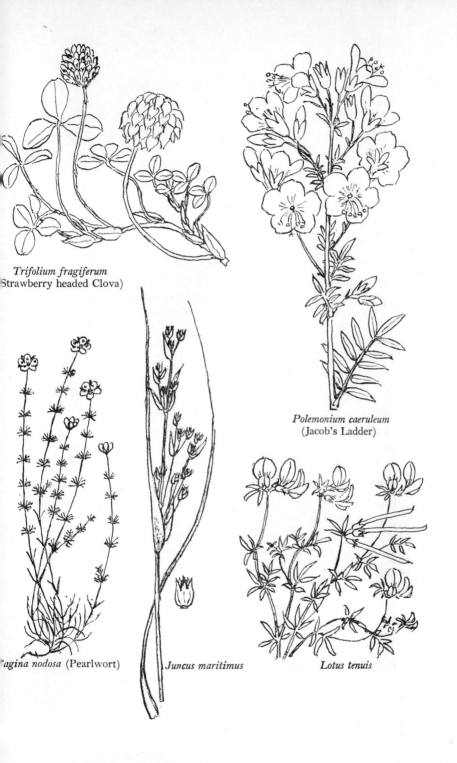

Trifolium fragiferum
(Strawberry headed Clova)

Polemonium caeruleum
(Jacob's Ladder)

agina nodosa (Pearlwort)   *Juncus maritimus*   *Lotus tenuis*

But somewhere about this time the *London Catalogue of British Plants* came into my hands, and this was marked off carefully into 100 sections, with usually about 15–20 names in each section, and this list became the guide to making the drawings into 100 plates. It was fairly easy to put an early drawing in some corner, and to fit those of related species beside them. This method led almost unawares to the plotting of the 100 plates of the *Concise British Flora*.

During my time at Lancaster, I was really overwhelmed with work and did practically no drawing.

✳ LANCASTER

I was duly licensed as senior curate of St. Mary's, Lancaster. This was the Mother Church of Lancaster with a population of about 10,000. The church is very large and was reputed to hold 1,400 on the ground floor. And there were large galleries filled with people from institutions or schools. Archdeacon Bonsey was the Vicar and Courtauld my fellow curate. There was a lay reader working at the Bulk Mission. One of the main industries was the production of linoleum at the Lune Works. The streets were cobbled and many families used a communal kitchen, so before midday there was a loud clattering of women's feet, all wearing wooden clogs, taking their meal to be cooked, and again about one o'clock fetching it. On one of the first Sundays, after preaching, I went to supper with the lay reader. We had apple tart (or apple pie you may call it), and he passed me a lump of cheese to go with it. I thought he was pulling my leg. I had never seen cheese with apple tart. I was told *all* North Country people had this. An area of visiting was allotted to me and

I took my turn as chaplain of the cemetery, i.e. for the town of 10,000. It was a shock to me to find sometimes three funerals arriving at the chapel at the same time.

The Bonseys were very kind to me and invited my fiancée on a short visit.

But this arrangement of the work did not last many weeks. Archdeacon Bonsey was taken ill in the late autumn and died. Courtauld, my fellow curate, then revealed that he had only come back to help temporarily, and that he was not licensed to the curacy or tied in any way, and he promptly left for work elsewhere. I was alone. Bishop Knox of Manchester came for the funeral of the Archdeacon. I rode with the Bishop to the cemetery in a smart carriage behind two rather frisky horses, rattling on the cobbles. We had not gone far before the left-hand horse put his leg over the pole and hopped along on three legs and was in danger of falling. We had to get out of the procession for a while.

On urgent appeal to the Bishop, he sent a temporary curate. But he was not in fit enough condition to take a full share in the work. The churchwardens, Mr. Satterthwaite and Mr. Seward, protested vigorously about this. There were 79 Confirmation candidates to be prepared, and a great number of sermons, and preparation took long in those days. We still have, 60 years later, the names of 79 young people and their record of attendance at classes. It meant four classes a week all through the winter 1908–9 with much visiting; in the church early every morning and up late in the evening, working something like 80 hours a week. The vitality of the curate was fully used. He had to write letters regularly to Ashbourne too, and paid two short flying visits by train, in the spring and summer after the Confirmation.

At Lancaster the church adjoins the Castle, where the figure of John of Gaunt stands over the gateway. And Lancaster was the county town, so the Law Sessions were held there. And the Session was preceded by a service in the Parish Church attended by the judge and others arrayed in wonderful gowns and big wigs. So it fell to my lot to be ready robed, and to bow to the judge in the church porch and to conduct him to the front pew, before I took the service. I like these dignified acts of politeness.

Bishop Knox came himself for Palm Sunday, Holy Week and Easter. He was a widower and I put him to lodge with a single lady in a big house near the church. So there was tittering over this. But the house was big and had a good domestic staff and was obviously best. I had handed the chaplaincies of the cemetery and of the hospital to other clergy but fulfilled that to the Loyal North Lancs. Regiment at the Barracks. I carried on till the first week of July 1909. Lancaster people were most generous in their gifts to me when I left. They presented me with a large silver tea and coffee set, of Queen Anne pattern, and a heavy silver salver.

* WATH

I was presented by the Dean and Chapter of Christ Church, Oxford, to the Benefice of Wath-on-Dearne. So I was married at Ashbourne on 8 July 1909.

After the strenuous time at Lancaster, I had of necessity a holiday, and it was also a honeymoon and the last place we stayed at was the Torcross Hotel on Slapton Sands. I introduced my wife to some of the birds on Slapton Ley. The D'Oyly Cartes were there at the same time. Fast motoring was new to us in those days (1909). Their holiday ended the same day as ours. And Mr. D'Oyly Carte kindly drove us, at what seemed a furious pace, to Dartmouth. He had a big car. Some of the bends in the road turned towards the sea, and it looked as though we should leap into the blue sea below us! but he was already a skilled driver. And we came safely to Wath-on-Dearne near Rotherham, in Yorkshire.

I had been warned that Wath would be a difficult parish. The Vicarage was condemned, and there was no building belonging to the Church where meetings of any kind could be held. The Old Vicarage had cracks an inch wide from the colliery workings. And we had to proceed to raise funds to build a new one. We used the old foundations, and kept the three cellars. Amongst the parochial records we found the original architect's plan of 1790. In this, the cellars were labelled for three kinds of ale. Adjoining it was the brew house. There was no tea or coffee in those days. And the Vicar was supposed to brew his own beer! We removed the brew house, and used the set pots, as dipping tanks for watering the garden, one of them under a tap. We soon found that this was not very safe for young children, who insisted on floating paper boats, and reaching across were liable to fall in head first. So the water had to be kept low.

But we had for the first year to live outside the parish at the top of West Melton, and to come in on foot or bicycle and back again three or more times a day, a considerable addition to labours. The new Vicarage was duly built and after much effort it was paid for; the patrons, the collieries and a local lawyer helping well. The parish of Wath was very short of buildings. Apart from the Parish Church there was no place where we could hold meetings of any kind. A sewing party had to hire a room at the Town Hall. Also the daughter Church of St. James badly needed a building for Sunday School and meetings. The Church Day School of Wath needed enlargement, otherwise we were soon to be threatened with dismissing 70 scholars. The Second Parish Church out at Adwick needed restoring. So I was destined to be a bricks-and-mortar parson. A lot of money had to be raised. I had none. There were two assistant curates, F. W. Botterill and D. T. Gabriel, but the fund which maintained them was in debt. Surely faithful work will produce the money from somewhere?

That second Parish Church at Adwick-on-Dearne was three miles away, usually reached by bike. The chancel of the church there was cut off from the nave by a heavy wall, with a very low arch hardly 6 feet wide. This needed opening up. It was terribly inconvenient whatever the archaeologists say, and the whole building needed restoring. This was duly done, a broad chancel arch was built and proved a great help.

The approach by road to Adwick Church was up a rather steep hill past Adwick gorse. One winter we had an inch of ice on the road from the end of November to the first week in March. It was necessary to bicycle on this ice repeatedly, even sometimes in rain. We had some good spills, owing to the wheel ruts in the ice, and when we came to the hill, we lifted the bike over the hedge and carried it on shoulder up a ploughed field. The alternative was hiring a horse cab to the bottom of the hill. No horse could get up it that winter.

On one occasion my wife and I were kindly invited to a ball at Wentworth Woodhouse by Lord Fitzwilliam; about midnight we left . . . and at the door the carriage before ours was announced by a footman as "Lady Alifax's carriage"—two smart horses, coachman and footman in uniform. Next it was "Vicar of Wath's carriage", a dirty old cab and a horse that looked nearly finished.

In the early days at Wath-on-Dearne very little was attempted in the way of flower drawing. We were both much occupied with the parish and the gardening. My wife was working up the Mother's Union. This was naturally interrupted sometimes when the family arrived. She was utterly loyal to me, helping with suggestions, or reminding me of omissions, and she had good friends in the parish. She did not yet realize that flower drawing would be a real recreation to me. One day in early summer I brought in a bit of common hedge mustard from the garden, and made a drawing of it. And while I was out at an appointment, she drew a rough clock on the sheet with the words "waste not, want not" above it, and adapted the tiny flower into a vicar in top hat and minute choir boys. So it had to be settled. I was brought up amid natural history, and was trained in botany, and now wild flowers were the one item of natural history available. And the occasional drawing of them was real recreation and most peaceful. My wife soon understood this. It also gave us an objective in going out sometimes to beautiful spots together.

We co-operated well in the work of those days. And there were other recreations together, such as gardening; we worked hard at that, especially at the kitchen garden. We had both been tennis players. For this last we had to make a tennis court, which took us two years. But, when provided, we could invite others now and then for tennis, making rare social occasions. There were, however, patches of clover on the court, which became slippery if at all damp. One day a principal local colliery director was playing, slipped on a clover patch and got up with the seat of his white tennis flannels as green as the grass, which caused amusement.

We believe that it was during the year 1911 that Dr. Johnston kindly drove me with my wife to the first flying meeting. This was held at Doncaster race-course. Blériot and the Wrights and others were making very short flights in aeroplanes rather like box kites, primitive biplanes in fact. There was quite a crowd beside the course, and we cheered Blériot and others when they managed to get up 100 feet. It was most dangerous for the crowd of spectators. They had scarcely any control of their machines, and a gust of wind might easily have landed them in the crowd. It is remarkable that in the summer of 1918, when the writer was a chaplain in France in the last year of the First World War, Air Force boys, if they had had a good run, sometimes looped the loop into the clouds before landing at the aerodrome. So quickly did war advance the power of flying. Necessity is indeed the mother of invention.

That same summer (1911) my wife and I were invited to a big garden party at Bishopthorpe by the Archbishop, Cosmo Gordon Lang. It was a lovely summer day, and there was a wonderful spread for the party. The Archbishop, good holy man, was very clever and was exceedingly kind to us. Again that summer the Archbishop came to stay a week-end with us. The men of Manvers Colliery had contributed liberally for a new church pulpit in memory of Mr. Thompson, their former general manager. The pulpit, designed by my brother, was beautifully carved. It had a nice figure of King Oswald, with sword in one hand and a cross in the other hand. He fought battles and preached the gospel. Wath Church had been for a good while in the past in the gift of St. Oswald's Priory at Nostell. The Archbishop dedicated this pulpit on the Sunday, and he also dedicated the new Church House, which was a valuable asset. At ten o'clock at night the Archbishop was sitting in the drawing-room, and my wife's great friend, Ida Askew, said, "Your Grace would you like to go to your room now, because we want to put the ducks to bed." We kept ducks and poultry in those days. And Ida Askew, the daughter of a former Vicar of Greystoke, was a splendid help. The children when they were small loved her and called her "Joe". She later became Mrs. McCullagh and we sometimes stayed with them near Ambleside and went for walks on the fells. She was a great fell walker.

Those were the days when there were girls in domestic service. There were plenty who were willing and anxious to come to the Vicarage. And they were very happy and loyal there. The wages were very small, but they got their good board and lodging, and the Vicar's income had to cover this. They also had good training in domestic work. Then when they knew how to run a house nicely, they were apt to get married, but sometimes they chose to stay with us even when we moved to a distance. This was the usual experience of such households at that time. We never bought vegetables, so we worked hard in the garden, and this was our main recreation. The gardener, nice man, Ashley, had to be dismissed as soon as we got there. He went to work for the local Council, and sometimes came into the paved back yard with horse and cart for ashes and rubbish, making a thundering noise. So when there was real thunder in the summer, the children said it was only Ashley's cartwheels.

We had learned to study quite a lot, in order to make sermons and class lessons really instructive. This study, and the consideration of its bearing on life, gave us useful thoughts in mind for the visiting. The first object of the visiting was to make friends with people, and to win their confidence by sympathy and mutual understanding. Then we could at least tell even those who were not members what the Church was thinking about that week. The visiting took long hours, and was real work. We prayed for guidance in it. And we certainly sometimes had clear conviction of having received it. We did also jot down the names and ages of the children, and code symbols of their relation to church membership.

Not far behind the Vicarage there was a canal, on which barges moved steadily in those days, and in front of the house there was a small grass paddock, where very soon we kept a donkey, which was presented to us. By that time we had two small children, aged 3 and 2, and we gave them rides in panniers on the donkey. Or sometimes a nursemaid did so. One day when she was in charge, the donkey, scared by traffic at a bridge, bolted furiously along the towing-path by the canal with the children, but fortunately it did not stumble.

Below the paddock and near the road were trees with many rooks' nests in spring time. One year when the rooks were busy at their nests, they were being frequently disturbed by stone throwing, and were very noisy. I decided to stop this. So one morning I rose from my studies and sprinted down there, out of sight to pounce on the boys. I threw myself into the arms of the young village policeman! He was throwing the stones. There were mutual apologies. And the rooks were at peace after that.

After the assistant curates, Botterill and Gabriel left, we had A. G. Shipley 1910–11, afterwards Vicar of Pontefract, and then E. E. Johnson at St. James's, and Maxwell Fisher, a deacon from Lincoln Theological College. The staff met in the Parish Church every morning at 8 a.m. for mattins and its lessons or earlier for Holy Communion. We had a Church Lads' Brigade, which had to be revived and instructed (a former member of it has written, 60 years later, to say that he remembers the Vicar coming back in uniform from France to talk to them). There were confirmation classes to be collected and taught. We revived a Communicants' Guild and gave suitable instruction. Archbishop Cosmo Gordon Lang, our diocesan bishop, had been a strong leader of the Church of England Men's Society. So in 1912 we started a branch. It became strong and produced some useful laymen's church work. My wife started the Mothers' Union which grew to a hundred members. This helped to keep the Vicar in touch with the mothers.

In May 1912 the Sheffield area was made into a diocese, and Leonard Burrows, dear good man, became our bishop. He often stayed with us, as we by that time had a good Church House for his meetings. He was a good bishop, a real friend and adviser to his clergy.

We tried to keep in touch with the men of the place both by visiting their homes and visiting their various works. This meant sometimes going down with them to the coal faces, especially the Barnsley seam and the Silkstone seam. The cage was driven by steam and descended at 60 miles an hour, or so we were told. It seemed that the floor just disappeared from under us, and then as it slowed the floor came up at such a pace that we found ourselves sitting on our heels. One day there was snow above ground and the thermometer stood at 84 degrees Fahrenheit down below. I believe the depth was roughly 5,000 feet.

Another sample was visiting the huge Wath Brewery, where we were shown all the various processes of the manufacture of beer. This place was large and served a wide area. It took some time to see it all, and then we had to go to the office, and of course drink their health in a pint of their beer. We usually knew the direction of the wind at night because we had the various smells of the brewery, the coke ovens or the Stanleys Soap Works. They made soap resembling Pears', semi-transparent, and supplied the Castle Liners with their product.

✳ THE FIRST WORLD WAR

What about those war days? It was a long period of all-out work, of visiting the homes of the large number called up, of earnest intercession in the churches, publishing monthly lists of those serving overseas. The district visitors helped with this. In the early days, before the rationing got going, there was a serious shortage of groceries in the local shops. It was a populous area. And we found one day that we had to go on bicycles to Doncaster (10 miles) to get sugar, margarine or fats for the children. But all church work was fully maintained and intensified. Everywhere the kind of idea that found expression was that by the war "members of the Church are warned to show forth to the world by their lives a more real self-sacrifice after the pattern of our Master". So there arose the National Mission, and additional effort to pass this warning to every house in the land. It was to be "a special effort to witness for God and His truth, a National Mission of Repentance and Hope". Our own Mission Week in Wath was 4–11 November. By that time the Vicar of Wath had already been sent on the Mission to three parishes, his place being filled on the Sundays. His first visit was to a rural parish with communicants from every household, the second a small town parish of good tradition. Then he was asked to go to a town parish of 22,000, said to have only half a dozen in the big church. So he asked the Bishop to commission six good Wath members as "Bishop's Messengers". We all met early each morning in church for Communion and tried to bring a few with us to a late evening service, and spent long days visiting. We hope it was at least some little help.

By the end of the summer of 1916 more than 600 men had gone into the forces from Wath. They were sad days indeed, as the number of bereavements increased. At that date we had not become accustomed to the idea of a parochial memorial, though familiar enough today. And in May 1917 it became necessary to refuse to erect private memorials for those who were killed, which some families who could afford it very much desired. It was their larger income which made them desire it. We were threatened with many wall tablets. The refusal was not very popular at the time. We had to say in our Magazine: "In the Parish Church there must be a worthy Memorial to all those who fall in the War, a scheme of some kind, which may add to the beauty and devotional character of this fine old Church, of which we act as trustees for future generations. We ask you therefore to wait, and even to bear with us, while we refuse to consent for a time to all private Memorials, for the good of the Church and of future generations." We little guessed what was ahead of us for that church building.

In 1916 Mr. Fisher left us and D. Nicoll-Griffith came as a deacon.

On Trinity Sunday, 3 June 1917, our junior curate, D. Nicoll-Griffith, was ordained priest. But immediately after this on 11 June he was sent, at the Bishop's urgent request, to St. Peter's, Abbeydale, Sheffield, a parish of 18,000, as the need of help there was very great. That Sunday, 10 June, we

Keble Martin watching birds at Dartington, *c.* 1897

Dartington Parsonage

The family at Dartington, 1898. Nuthatches nested in the ivy-covered
wall on the left

The Church at Wath-on-Dearne, Yorks, 1913, before the fire and showing the pulpit

The pulpit at Wath Church, with figure of King Oswald. 500 miners subscribed to this, and it was dedicated in 1911 by Dr. Cosmo Lang, then Archbishop of York. The benefice was for a long while in the gift of St. Oswald's Priory at Nostel

Dora Martin, the author's
mother, at Ottery St. Mary,
c. 1912

Violet Martin, with Patrick
and Barbara, 1912

held a United Sunday School Festival, that is of all the Sunday
Schools in Wath, long processions to the Town Hall grounds
for a United Service, an ecumenical effort, which became
annual. Even the Church of England Sunday Schools, teachers
and scholars together numbered over a thousand.

Our own Sunday School Treat was held in fine weather on
Thursday, 17 August. We were all away on a field above the
Church House. Soon after 5 p.m. a message reached me that
the Parish Church was on fire. "Then who has done it?" I
exclaimed, getting hurriedly on a bicycle. There had been no
heating or lighting for many weeks. When I got to the church
the inside of the vestry was red hot, and flames were pouring
out of its windows and through a doorway up to the chancel
roof. A kind neighbour, Mr. Kay, had already rescued some
ornaments from the sanctuary at some risk to himself, altar
cross and candlesticks and hangings. The fire hydrants were
slow in getting to work. The first was turned on at about
5.30. The situation was then looking desperate. The chancel
roof was a mass of flames, which streamed westward throughout the carved sixteenth-century nave roof. Kind friends
fought to prevent the organ from blazing. Our hose was taken
through the broken east window. Others were got going and
by 6.15 the fire was under control. Many kind people worked
hard and were soaked to the skin; but no one was injured,
though there were some narrow escapes from falling tiles.
Seventy-five thousand gallons of water were used, or so we
were told. The metal pipes of the organ were melted, and
wooden pipes were filled with water and were falling to
pieces. Two little piles of sticks were found behind the organ
with burnt out matches beside them. They failed to light up.

For two nights the building was watched. On Saturday an
army of willing workers wheeled barrow loads of tiles,
charred wood and mud out of the sanctuary. What remained
of the chancel roof was covered with borrowed tarpaulins.
The whole floor of the church was scrubbed and all the pews.
The carved oak altar was scorched and black, and had to be

washed. The ornaments and hangings were replaced, and the church was used for worship on that Sunday (20 August).

It was realized that no effective repairs or rebuilding could be undertaken at that time, as no licence could be obtained for materials until the war was over. This delay provided opportunity for fuller consideration of what improvements, if any, should be attempted. It also helped to solve the problem of a suitable church war memorial.

Six weeks after the fire it was still not known who had caused it. The Vicar was determined to discover this. It was found that one boy was not on the School Treat field, and that he was seen near the church about that time. A few days previously the organist choirmaster had called him a dirty little brute, and possibly smacked him. The fire was a terrible act of revenge. Having failed to set fire to the organ, he put a match to the surplices in the vestry. He was taken to court at Rotherham and confessed it. He was not whipped for it, but was sent to a Reformatory for five years.

At this time, 1917, our family consisted of Patrick (age 6), Barbara (age 5), Vivienne (age 4) and Henry the baby. We took them over to Bolton-on-Dearne to see a little bomb hole made by a Zeppelin on its way to Sheffield Steel Works. It had been only a shrapnel bomb for dropping in camps and the hole was quite small. Patrick said he could have dug a bigger hole himself. In the early days of 1918 Henry was just able to pull himself up beside the music stool, admiring his mother at the piano.

✳ ARMY CHAPLAINCY

In the winter of 1917–18 there was an urgent call for more chaplains with the army overseas. I had an able curate, Eric Parker, and two neighbouring vicars were willing to co-

operate in maintaining church services at Wath. So I volun-
teered to go overseas as a temporary Chaplain to Forces.
And the Bishop agreed. There was an intense course of training for eight days at Tidworth, on Salisbury Plain. When I
arrived at the entrance of it, I was caught by the arm with
the exclamation: "We have got him" and was passed on to
the Commandant. I asked what he thought I had done. "Oh,
nothing: you are my student No. 10,000." I was presented
with an inscribed First Aid book at a lecture next morning.

With intervals for meals and exercise, the lectures lasted
from 7 a.m. to 11 p.m. daily. The exercise was doubling
round the quadrangle in full equipment. We even learned
how to make tea and to pour it into another kitty after four
minutes for the others coming in later. I reported at Army
Headquarters at Cassell, a hill-top where six roads meet, and
had to go and hunt for my battalion, 34th Northumberland
Fusiliers, who were out of touch after retreating. My first
day with them was on a front line where they had been
through long and hard fighting. "Here's your horse, sir," a
man said. "Oh, take it away please and bring me a push-bike"
(I had driven plenty but not ridden). But the battalion was
soon moved to a rest camp, so there were a few days of active
visiting among them, and a voluntary service in a hut packed
with men. This was just in time, as the next day the enemy
offensive was renewed, and conditions changed completely.
But we were usually able to hold services either out of doors,
or in tents or barns, my good batman carrying a knapsack
full of service books. During a few days of rest, an accurate
casualty list was compiled. And the chaplain took over the
writing of letters to the next of kin, writing for hours on some
packing case in a draughty barn.

On the Sundays the battalion was either in the line or on
the march. So the only Sunday services were held very early
in the morning with loins girt for a march. It was a privilege
to have shared even for a short while the dangers of life at the
front, and the unpleasantness of forward billets, often barns

with straw full of uninvited guests. The Chaplain wrote to his Parish Magazine at home to say: "Do not make any mistake, the men long intensely for cleanliness and home, but there is a most noble spirit of self-sacrifice and endurance abroad. And they will stick to it. *Pray* for them. Under immense danger much brotherly kindness is being shown. Another side to it is that the birds are in full song and the flowers in full bloom. They are all our own familiar friends, the sweet English birds and flowers, robins buttercups and daisies and others, reminding us how very near the fighting is to our own dear homes."

Looking back I remember that the dykes near the Belgian border were later on just like gay flower-beds. The water was covered with those gay flowers on Plate 79 of the *Concise British Flora*, and we hardly ever met with non-British flowers, any more than we do in England. The flora was the same as in England. But we are anticipating. We are still in late spring.

At this time I was receiving sad letters from my home at Wath. My younger son, now aged 2, was very ill with meningitis, the result of falling off his mother's bed. He fell on his head. And about the end of May I was given compassionate leave to visit my home. Arriving in Yorkshire in the early morning and walking into Wath from Swinton station at 6 a.m., I met the good road foreman, who expressed sympathy with me on my son's death. I did not tell him that I had not heard of it till that moment. I was full of thought for my wife. But my coming was a relief to her and she wept. She had done her utmost for him and was tired. Patrick had lost his younger brother too. After that little funeral, we moved the family down to Ottery St. Mary, Devon, where my mother and sisters lived, taking a small place in Silver Street.

Then I returned to France and to my unit. The battalion had suffered heavy losses in the retreats, and on one of the first hot days, we were taken out of the line and marched back 21 kilometres, carrying full equipment. There were boys of poor physique in the army at the end of the war. So the Padre and often other officers were usually carrying rifles on long marches.

Soon after this I was re-posted, as an Army Corps chaplain, and amongst other things it fell to my duty to visit a number of young men at cross-roads and bridges, bridge guards in fact. They had a dangerous task, as the enemy had all these spots measured, and they shelled them continually. Many of them were killed at their posts of duty. I visited many of them and one day practically all those, that I had seen, were former Church of England choir boys. So they knew the hymns and prayers of the Church. Boys' choirs had been large in those days.

At the end of the summer I was at a busy spot in a back area. We had church services in a football pavilion or in a Church Army hut, and one service each Sunday out of doors, the remains of three battalions present and sometimes a choir of nurses from hospital barges. We had no loud speaker, only an effort of voice production. Communicants mostly came at 6.30 in the morning, also often after evensong, because men were on duty in early morning and there were always units going up to the line on Sunday night, the area being partly a rest camp. This area was quite different from that of the former area that I was in during April and May. And there were some sad men there who had been out a long time, and whose wives were not faithful. War is terribly destructive of family life.

In the autumn we all moved forward, and things seemed much better. William Temple, later Archbishop, came and talked to us. One Sunday near the Lys river, moving from one service to another, I saluted King George V all alone. At the Armistice time we were at Vambrachies. It was wet weather, and further losses kept occurring through road mines exploding. I stayed out through the winter, running such things as a Corps Cinema, to help keep idle men out of mischief. The winter was cold, my batman filled a rubber bath with water overnight and I had to break the ice each morning.

At last we were demobilized and back at Wath, and able to prepare for the restoration of the church. This was duly accomplished at last. We had to raise a lot of money for the restoration. The east window became the parochial Church War Memorial.

While the Vicar was still away, that is in February 1919, the first ten pages of the Wath History were printed in the Parish Magazine without his knowledge. But the whole was accomplished afterwards. Some years earlier Mr. Gawtress had handed the Vicar a whole big sackful of very old deeds, dating back to about 1300, and mostly referring to lands in Wath. This was rather a challenge. Some of the deeds were in Latin or partly in Latin and partly in French, with words much abbreviated and letters quite differently formed from those nowadays. These "musty old deeds" as my wife called them, had often been pulled out the last thing at night, especially during long winter evenings. Then I used some Yorkshire Archaeological Society sources, as I was a member. And the *History of Wath-on-Dearne* was published by Messrs. Farthing in 1919 and received good commendation from Yorkshire archaeologists. I remember that in early days in Wath, a sheep cost "fower pence", so the present devaluation of money is nothing new.

In the years immediately following the War we were very busy at Wath, revisiting the whole parish and getting the church restored. My curate, Eric Parker, got preferment and the Rev. A. E. Appleton came to Wath. Life was much influenced at this time by the presence of our small children. My eldest, Patrick, was much away at a boarding school at Malvern, and two daughters attended a small day school in Sandygate and were much at home. They had some kind grown up friends. Dr. Johnston's sister known as "Jonty", and Mr. Muspratt, one of Mr. Nicholson's legal staff. He was a bachelor, fond of children, and he came in often to talk to them or bring them children's papers or sweets. A third daughter, Lisette, born 1919, was barely two years of age when we left Wath. At the age of one, unable to walk, she escaped notice one day, and punted herself down the gravel drive, through the open gate and some distance up the pavement of the busy Barnsley Road, where by that time the traffic was heavy. At last a kind neighbour brought her back with no seat left to her trousers. By the late summer of 1921 she could walk, and loved to go down the shrubbery, where much wild cow parsley flower was level with her head. So when I got home she had learned to say "Down here Daddy", and we often went.

All that hot summer of 1921 my second daughter— Vivienne, aged 7, was ill, and was on her back by day in a basket bed on wheels in the garden. We took her meals out to her, and on one day we thought she had done well in eating milk pudding. But later on we saw it scattered in the currant bushes. Her illness however made me convinced that my resolution to move to a less smoky district was a right one for the children's sake.

✳ HACCOMBE AND COFFINSWELL

The summer of 1921 was very dry and sunny. And this fine weather coincided with a colliery strike. The miners had been needing a good holiday. We met them pouring out from a pit into the sunshine. They were shouting to their friends; "We eint goin to do nowt for a moonth" and we sympathized with them. So that summer the Pennine hills were clearly visible. We only saw them during strikes.

The writer had been Vicar of Wath for about twelve years. And a member of his family was seriously ill all the summer.

It happened that Miss Carew of Haccombe near Torquay had offered him the benefice of Haccombe and Coffinswell. He went down to see her at Marley House near South Brent, and accepted the offer. The family were to live at Coffinswell. His brother had been there before him. And the move was timed for the last week of July. The grass on the fields and lawns was brown and dry. But just as the furniture arrived at the rectory, the sky opened up. We had a drenching thunder-storm, water everywhere. The little Rectory drive was made of gravel bedded in stiff yellow clay. And this was trodden freely to every corner of the newly scrubbed house. And all had to be scrubbed again.

The place was attractive. There was a large garden which had to be maintained. That was good exercise. There was a tennis court recently made by my brother. This was useful for the family. The hill pastures of Haccombe had nice wild flowers and hares. I was duly instituted as Archpriest of Haccombe and Rector of Coffinswell by Bishop Cecil of Exeter. I continued in that office for $12\frac{1}{2}$ years, and was always alone for a daily office in the church at Coffinswell at 8 a.m. except on festivals, yet not always quite alone. While reading the psalms and lessons aloud which I found helpful; small winged visitors frequently came and joined in. There was a rat hole under the tower door and the local robins and wrens knew all about it, and came to clear insects or spiders from the windows, and then sometimes sat on the pulpit near me to sing loudly, as if to drown my voice. There was then actually a Jenny Wren singing within six feet of the surpliced figure of the Rector! The wrens also came in to Haccombe Church and built a nest in the carving under the pulpit. We have for 45 years had the habit of tolling the church bell at 8 in the morning, sometimes with a curate or two and often alone. We have reminded members that there is some prayer for the parish in the church at that time. And the bell may be regarded as an angelus, and they can throw up a prayer at their work in the fields. The slow reading aloud led to useful consideration of meaning and application to present day life, especially if we remembered to look up the passages in a commentary overnight.

But I had been accustomed for many years to the visiting of large populations. And now within a very short time I had visited all my new parishioners once or twice. And the amount of Church ministration called for was much less. So I soon found that I had not enough to do. Taking pupils who were preparing for the university was not a success. The flower drawing advanced rapidly. All the drawings on the first twelve plates at least were made in this period, but it was only a recreation. Indeed in these early days of our time at Coffinswell we were free to take good holidays. Sometimes it was while the children were away at school. Thus in the summer of 1923 my wife and I went in June to visit my eldest brother at Hunsdon Mill, Herts, a house belonging to the Gibbs family, where my brother had a market garden. There we met Miss Trower of Stanstead Abbots who painted flowers very beautifully, we exchanged a few ideas, and the Common Meadow Rue (Pl. 1) was drawn. Again in July we went to the Lizard and added *Geranium sanguineum* and *Genista pilosa* (Pl. 21). Similarly in 1924 we

Thalictrum flavum (Meadow Rue)

visited Berry Head, not far away, for the White Rock Rose
and other local plants, and watched some Black Redstarts on
the cliffs. In this and the following year we paid short visits
to kind friends at Bacton-on-sea on the Norfolk coast, and a
serious effort was made to get some plants peculiar to the
Norfolk Broads. Hiring a light skiff on Bridge Broad,
Cardamine amara (Pl. 7) and the prettily curved *Carex pseudo-*
cyperus (Pl. 94) were added. This last led to trouble. The best
clump of it which I made for, happened to be near a swan's
nest. And both the swans attacked me fiercely with their long
beaks, flapping of their great wings and screaming. There
was difficulty in keeping the sculls out on the water, and that
is necessary in a skiff. I did not want to roll over, but after a
few minutes I got away with my *Carex*. And our kind hostess
Mrs. Granville provided a tower
room where some drawing could
be done without interruption,
before returning to Coffinswell.

At about this date a letter was
written to the Bishop of Sheffield
offering to come back to any
industrial parish in the Sheffield
Diocese provided that there was a
reasonable house for the family,
but there was no parish vacant
just at that time. There was some
result however two years later.

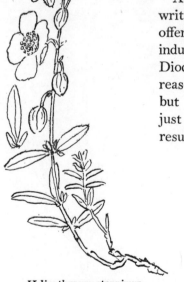

Helianthemum apenninum
(White Rock Rose)

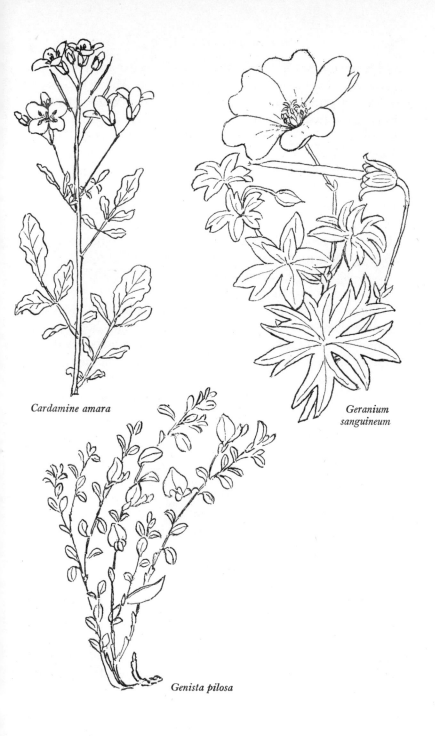

Cardamine amara

Geranium sanguineum

Genista pilosa

Meanwhile we not only seemed to be called upon for more preaching work, but bicycling to Newton Abbot we found ourselves continually passing some new houses which appeared in Addison Road near the Torquay high road at Milber. The houses were being built by a Development Company for the Newton Abbot Urban District Council, but they were in the ecclesiastical parish of Combe-in-Teignhead. Mr. Pound the Rector of Combe-in-Teignhead was elderly. And the only means of transport that he possessed was an old pony which he rode, but it was not suitable for visiting a housing estate three miles away over two steep hills. So we offered to do the visiting. The Rector gladly agreed and also Bishop Cecil.

So I visited them in the summer of 1926. Thus the work in Milber had its small beginning.

Meanwhile we had a happy family circle at home. We gardened and played tennis during the summer holidays. In winter we also tobogganed on the steep Haccombe pastures. One of the toboggans always upset and was known as the little demon.

When the children were home from school at about this period, especially in the end of the summer holidays, we were allowed by Sir Henry Carew to take pony and dray and collect loads of logs in some of his woods. This made splendid recreation for us all. It was working together. I believe my wife and family particularly enjoyed these little trips.

In the winter evenings of 1932–33, serious consideration was given to the possibility of completing the one hundred painted plates of flowers, a careful estimate was made of the work done and the work undone, and a statement was written on the recent progress. After a careful survey of the work this showed that out of about 1,480 figures proposed, only 677 or less than half had been drawn. And that whereas in 1927 some 66 figures had been added, in 1932 only 24 were drawn. The amount of new work added in each year had thus fallen, very much. This was partly due to the extra parochial work at Milber. But I wrote "we do not wish to change that". It was also partly due to the repainting of earlier plates. The paper used at first was of poor quality and became seriously discoloured. And since 1924 all the work had been redrawn and repainted on better paper. In copying plates each figure had to be traced on to thin paper first, and retraced. "The longest way round was the shortest way home." The slowing up of progress was also partly due to the difficulty of obtaining the rarer species. So in addition to my own efforts, lists of desired species were issued to members of the Botanical Exchange Club, and several members responded nobly. Often a first drawing was made from a posted specimen, improved later from my own gathering.

Thus the figures on the plates, as we see them, were not always completed in a single effort. To look at the first plate only, and the little figure at the top. *Thalictrum alpinum* was first drawn from a specimen gathered on Ben Lawers in Perthshire by Mr. Helsby in 1927. In the following year I saw it on Widdebank fell, a leaf was added and the figure much improved. Then the whole place was traced, retraced and repainted in 1932. This was the story in many cases. How to do the work had to be learned the harder way by experience, without help. Thus the better quality of foliage green was discovered by accident in 1930. Cobalt blue was upset on white paper and later some aureolin yellow was upset partly over the blue. There was a bright leaf green. The one colour must dry first.

In 1933, my last full year at Coffinswell and Milber, a lot of parochial work was called for, more visiting, more sermons and class teaching, more meetings. Very little flower drawing was done, but the beauty of nature was all around. Going to my visiting at Milber I sometimes walked the top way by Conybear and down the public path through the wood. And there in early summer there were always Wood Wrens singing; a very local bird with a soft sibilant song, but peaceful. I watched their beaks quivering, and the Padre went from that to his visiting.

Then as a family we had some nice little outings to the coast, and a holiday together to Gara Rock near Thurlestone. There was an old Coast Guard station here, turned into a small boarding house. The seaside birds were a great attraction, and several uncommon plants were added.

There was also a hurried visit to Perthshire. After a full Sunday, 24 July 1933, the midnight train took me to Killin and Ben Lawers. There the clouds were down to 1,000 feet. I went straight up in the clouds and rain and chanced to find two nice Saxifrages, one especially which is very local and flowers sparingly. It was in flower. I took it down and made a drawing and coloured it. The next morning, up in mist and rain again, I luckily found its own niche, and replanted it firmly in its own place. A few other little alpine species were gathered, and these were in cigarette tins. They were all drawn in the train during Thursday night on the return journey. I was sorry to have had to go without my wife. At a later date, she was free to go there with me. And the story will appear later.

Again, that September, Mr. H. W. Pugsley, the expert on Fumitories, took me round West Cornwall in his car, visiting the best localities for collecting Fumitories (Pl. 6). So I was lucky. Holidays were brief but very effective.

At Coffinswell Church we had managed to get the ceiling of the sanctuary remade under the direction of Mr. Herbert Read. And the Rector had kept the grass in the churchyard mown as far as possible with a lawn mower. It seemed to happen that people sometimes arrived to see him just when he was busy mowing. He had also made an effort to clean off the heavy whitening of the ancient stone font. And working with very strong soda had taken no less than 36 pieces of skin off his hands in doing it.

At one time old Lord Kinsale lived at Homefield, opposite the Rectory at Coffinswell, and being a director of the Moran Tea Co. in Assam, he persuaded my son Patrick to prepare for tea planting by going first for two years' training in engineering with the Crossley Engine Works in Manchester. Lord Kinsale was afterwards failing in health and we had to visit him regularly. He was very cheerful. And only a few days before he died, he enjoyed telling me this story. He was reading his Bible in the train. A stranger opposite him asked him: "Excuse me, sir, but do you believe in that book you are reading?"

Kinsale: "Oh yes, I do indeed."

Stranger: "Well I don't believe a word of it."

Kinsale: "I am sorry."

Stranger: "What about Jonah: do you believe he recited a poem in the belly of the whale? Is that true?"

Kinsale: "Well, when I get to paradise I will ask him."

Stranger: "Supposing he is not there?"

Kinsale: "Then *you* can ask him!"

There was an old chap down the village, old Mr. Ryder, a retired farm worker. He lived opposite the "Stoggy Marsh" at the bottom of the village. We had to visit him when he was failing. He liked to talk about the gardening, and he several times said: "Oe them weeds when them is small." We had mainly to illuminate Bible teaching in sermons; but we did sometimes quote old Ryder's words in reference to bad habits. They are also easier to hoe in early stages.

Visiting sick folk, with all that this includes, is useful work. It serves at least to cheer and encourage them and prayer for restoration is very real. In one case a man who had both legs completely paralysed for more than a year, said one day that he felt a little tingling in his toes. A little later he was walking and working like other men.

*   *   *

* DARFIELD

When we had just nicely started the visiting of Milber, the work there was interrupted for a while, because in the early autumn of 1926 the Bishop of Sheffield (Dr. Leonard Burrows) asked me to exchange for six months with Canon Sorby, the Vicar of Darfield near Barnsley who was needing a rest. Darfield was a parish of 11,000 pop. with two churches. And I undertook this exchange with Bishop Cecil's permission. So we travelled back to Yorkshire, aiming at doing at least a thousand visits (or 40 a week) in addition to other fairly arduous duties. We arrived in Yorkshire by train with our youngest daughter on the evening of 5 November. In the Sheffield area the whole countryside was lighted up with bonfires.

We were now suddenly planted in the big Rectory house at Darfield, wondering how best to serve both its Parish Church and the daughter church of Houghton. Almost the next day a priest from Saskatchewan, N. Canada named George Turner landed in Liverpool. He went straight to the telephone and speaking to the Bishop of Sheffield asked for work in his Diocese. The Bishop told him to go to Martin at Darfield and he arrived the next day with his wife. We worked hard and loyally together throughout our stay in Darfield and were wonderfully happy. Mr. Turner was duly licensed to the curacy, and he mostly looked after Houghton a large daughter district, and its church.

In addition to the normal church services there was a big Bible class on Sunday afternoons taken by the pro-Rector. And it grew from about 70 members to more than 100. This was largely due to the strike which then prevailed. There had been a "general strike" in the summer of 1926 and the colliery aspect of it lasted much longer.

The churchyard at Darfield was overgrown with elders, brambles and nettles and the young men of the Bible class

working with me on week days, cleared away several loads
of these elders and brambles getting one side of it down to
control even with a lawn mower by the time we left in the
following May. The visiting and other work had to be maintained meanwhile. But we enjoyed working together when
possible. And they were glad to harden their hands, which
were soft, owing to the long strike. And they found a happiness in doing a voluntary work, that is unpaid work for the
Church.

There was a strong Girl Guide group, and we dedicated a
banner for them. This was run by Miss Elmhirst, the
daughter of a Barnsley vicar. Her father and mother came to
study my flower drawings at Darfield Rectory. It is a curious
coincidence that their son, who had been living in America,
was somewhere near that time purchasing Dartington our
old home in Devon.

There was a large garden at Darfield Rectory, and on the
lawn our children fed the hedgehogs with bread and milk. And
in the holidays we played hockey there together with the
maids, (Lizzie and Ida) who spoke broad Yorkshire. A
daughter told me one day that Lizzie says she "has putten the
shugger in the cooberd" but one local pronunciation may be
as expressive as another. We were all happy working in
Darfield and returned in May 1927 to Coffinswell.

* COFFINSWELL AND MILBER

So in the summer of 1927 the visiting of Milber was continued. They had no very near place of worship. So cards
were printed recording hours of worship at all the neighbouring churches and these cards were taken to every house. There
was the usual happiness in getting to know people, but as

4

there was no Sunday work to prepare for Milber, life was
not arduous. And other studies advanced, both flower drawing
and the history of the parish of Coffinswell. This history of
Coffinswell was published by the Devonshire Association
more than 20 years later. And this led to a very human mis-
understanding, because in the last six lines I had departed
from history, and suggested that an improvement should be
made in the entrance to the church, for the 800th Anniversary
(1959). This was written in 1927. The people concerned and
of course the Rector, had changed before the suggestion was
even published. They all thought it had been written yester-
day, that is in 1953! And the interfering author was asked
never to enter Coffinswell again.

Various botanical walks, mostly of Devon Association
members were conducted in suitable areas. Often this involved making a preliminary visit to find samples of less
common species. The walks were quite good fun. The conductor's naming of a plant settled all dispute!

Crossing Milber Down one day in early summer I came
upon a lovely great buzzard trapped in a gin, which had been
baited with a rabbit. His beak looked very fierce, and his
great wings were spread widely on the heather, I put my foot
on the gin and released him. His leg was evidently painful
and for a few seconds he did not realize he was free. Then he
flew over the keeper's cottage to throw down an anathema.
I ran home and typed a note saying it was illegal to destroy
these birds at that season and signed it only in type script:
"Fellow of the Linnean Society of London". The gamekeeper
worked for my Patron. Did he guess who the villain was that
let the great bird go free? There were obvious buzzard
feathers on the trap, so he knew the bird was caught.

In the year 1927 the Torquay Corporation were wishing
to extend their boundaries and to include much of Coffinswell
in Torquay, widening roads and constructing pavements.
This would have destroyed many wild flowers, before it was
necessary. A public meeting about this extension was held in

Torquay in November. The writer sat through the meeting with Eden Phillpots, a well known lover of rural Devon. I had often had occasion to travel from my work near Sheffield to see my parents in South Devon, after Easter for instance. And I told the meeting that my fellow travellers often said that they came to Torquay, because they liked to see the primroses in the lanes around. This was true enough, but the statement was not appreciated in Torquay. The town extension was however defeated.

The new housing estate at Milber Newton Abbot was being built by a Development Company and in the year 1928 this company offered a small site as a free gift for a church. They called Bishop Cecil of Exeter, and he actually came with the Rector of Combe. The site had a small gravel pit in it, and was not nearly large enough. I could do nothing but shake my head: "Not good enough". This incident provoked me into applying to the Earl of Devon for a better site, meeting him and his agent Mr. Gardiner at Powderham. He was the main Milber land owner. He responded willingly, and offered two acres for £300. We consulted the Newton Abbot Town Planning Officer regarding probable extension. And we chose the two acre site on which the church and vicarage now stand, the Rector and the Bishop agreeing to this site. Mr. Gardiner, the agent came and pegged out the corners, and dear Mr. Ellicott who had a market garden at Penn Inn Corner in Milber came and marked it out with a small plough.

There was no big room to meet in, so at midsummer we held an outdoor whist-drive under an oak tree at the top of the church field, but it became chilly towards the end! In September we held a fête by kind invitation of Col. and Lady Amy Bertie a sister of Lord Devon at Forde House. This is a wonderful historic house in which royal persons have stayed. This was the first real effort to raise funds for that new church. Amongst other things a quantity of pencils were sold, inscribed "Milber Church Site Fête, Nineteen hundred and twenty eight". This was followed by a second fête at the

same house the following year, opened by Lady Caroline
Courtenay, with a good stirring speech. People did work
hard; A sewing party of 20 members met every week at Mr.
Ellicott's house.

But during these years 1927-29 when the preparations for
the Milber Church were proceeding there were no Sunday
services at Milber and the amount of parochial work called
for was still less than we were accustomed to. And these
years saw some rapid advance in the drawing of flowers.
At midsummer 1927 my wife and I went by train to Teesdale
and on from there to Ambleside. At the former we saw the
Globe Flower, *Trollius* (Pl. 4) at its best, and *Rubus saxatilis*
(Pl, 29) and others. At Ambleside the tuberous Comfrey

Trollius europaeus (Globe Flower)

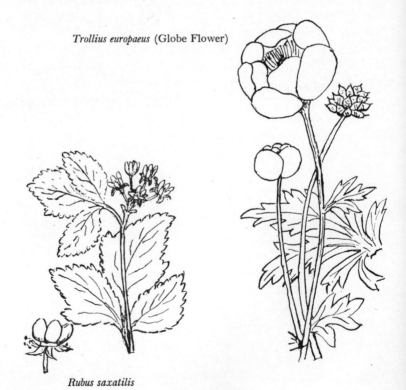

Rubus saxatilis

Gentiana verna

Trifolium strictum

Symphytum officinale (Comfrey)

(Pl. 60) was seen and others which were drawn in the train. During that August Sir Henry Carew lent us an empty game-keeper's cottage at Shipley Bridge near Brent. So we took the family with camp beds and cooking materials and with a food supply for a holiday, and a few Dartmoor bog plants were drawn.

In 1928 after collecting tithe at Quethiock we took a short holiday in mid-June at the Lizard. And the floating Marsh-Wort (Pl. 37) and four small trefoils (Pl. 22) were added. Then a little later, we went again to Teesdale and to

Cumberland, about ten other local plants were drawn including *Gentiana verna, Primula farinosa* (Pl. 57) and the Water Lobelia (54). Long periods of steady work preaching and visiting intervened between these holidays.

Primula farinosa

In 1929 two local species of Heath Violets were drawn, one of them close to the new houses on Milber Down, to preserve its memory after destruction. This was the tall form of *Viola canina*, since figured by Miss Grierson on the stamps (1967). Then in early June my wife and I again went to collect the Haccombe tithe from Quethiock in Cornwall. So we took the opportunity of going on to St. Ives, where two local Fumitories (Pl. 6) were collected and drawn and the Cornish Figwort (Pl. 63) on June 6 and 7th. I was painting these at 6 a.m.

And on 27 June I went by train to Weston-super-Mare, and hired a small boat with an outboard motor, and its owner with a very weathered face. Having persuaded him to take me across to Steepholme Island, I had a delightful hour or two on the cliffs there, choosing suitable specimens of the Paeony (Pl. 4) and some Stonecrops. Then when we started on the return trip the little chain of the motor broke. It was a poor little thing like a cheap bicycle chain. There were no oars (I was accustomed to rowing) and as the tide was running out very fast, we sped helplessly past Worle Head towards Lundy Island heading I suggested for New York. Though of course we should have come back more or less at about 2 a.m. I found some string in my pocket, with which the chain was mended, and it lasted long enough to get us back to Weston.

* MILBER

These easier years came to an end, and in February 1930 a wooden Mission Room was opened at Milber and licensed by the Bishop. This was a dual purpose building for worship, with a small sanctuary which could be shut off: and also for social meetings, because social gatherings have their proper and essential place in church life. There was a raised platform in front of the sanctuary. And at the opening we arranged for Lord Devon (and others) to be seated there: he was pretty well eclipsed by the large surpliced figure of Archdeacon Cobham. The Bishop in his address said "These are the days of small things. There was a lot of work to do here".

From this date church services were held here in Milber and a Sunday School. And we wrote in the Parish Magazine: "With such a team of workers, inspired by loving co-operation, we shall bear our financial responsibilities with light hearts". We were well in debt, both for the site and for the Mission Room. During the first Lenten season I gave some addresses on St. Luke, after which the Church Council asked that the future church should be called St. Luke's.

From this date February 1930 we had to hold church services and to preach at Milber in addition to the same at Haccombe and Coffinswell. Sunday was therefore a very full day, often there were seven services, the first at 7.30 a.m. at Coffinswell and the last Evensong at 7 p.m. at Milber. And as there were now services on Easter Day they were allowed by the Rector to give Easter Offerings to the Curate-in-charge, which more than covered the cost of extra travelling.

For about eight years the work at Milber was voluntary or unpaid work except for this annual offering after 1930. We had no idea of suggesting that the work should be paid for. Not that it was a case of a rich man being well able to give his services. In this and the three following years, it was not easy. In spite of frugal living, the bank account was, more often than not, overdrawn, with all that this involved in the way of pledges to the bank. We saw the need for work at Milber and the opportunity of doing it. And this was surely a call to fulfil it. It would have been wrong not to have done it. So it was no work of supererogation as somebody called it. Voluntary work becomes a deep source of happiness for us all. And a large part of the work which we do as Christians is of this nature. The calling was plain. In the Parish Magazine of May 1930 we quoted the opening words of the 115th Psalm: "Not unto us etc." adding: "Let this be our thought."

Soon after this the Padre tried to check the bad behaviour of some young people from the town, and there arose an element of personal opposition in some quarters though not among Milber Church members. This opposition was reflected in a remarkably clear dream in March 1931. I was preaching in a new church building from the chancel step. The church was filled with people, and was of a curious pattern. The altar stood in a round stone apse behind me. There were three diverging naves in front of me, one unfinished. A man came up from the centre to assault me. The warden and sidesmen came promptly and apprehended him, they conducted him down the North nave which was full of people, and cast him into the outer darkness. When the congregation had left I walked out by the central nave, and could see through the arches into the lateral nave. This curious pattern in a very vivid dream was at once submitted to my architect brother Arthur, who pronounced it quite feasible. And when he had drawn it, the Milber Church Council unanimously adopted

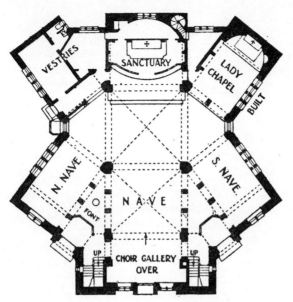

Plan of the Milber Dream Church

the plan. The Diocesan Advisory Council accepted it, and in spite of the Second Great War it has now been built. One advantage of it seemed to be that the altar and the celebrant are close to the people and can be seen from every pew.

Although we still had, as yet, only the wooden Mission Room, we found that our worship together gave us greater mutual confidence, and a happy spirit of true fellowship. By 1932 both the two acre site and the Mission Room were fully paid for. The dream is recorded on a foundation stone outside the Lady Chapel.

✳ CLOVA

We referred to a one day trip to Steepholme Island in June 1929 (p. 102). And in the August of that year there was a quick journey by train between Sundays to the Clova Mountains in Scotland. After the midnight of a busy Sunday the 1.15 a.m. train took me from Newton Abbot sleeping soundly all the way to Edinburgh. Thence to Kirrimuir. I knew little about distances there, and proceeded to walk with raincoat and baggage to Milton-of-Clova. The distance, we believe is 20 miles or more. Fortunately a coal lorry came along with a generous lift. And after delivering coal at several farms, we arrived at Milton-of-Clova. Three days were spent in rapid walks on the mountains. Many August flowering alpine plants were found, and also the kind co-operation of Mr. Corstorphine of Inchdowrie. The twelve alpine species included *Astragalus alpinus*, which had been declared extinct there for the past eight years. There was plenty of it, waving its slender purple heads, where only the bees, the birds and the angels could reach it as I told him. At a later date Mr. Corstorphine was persuaded to drag himself up there to see it. In one house where kind hospitality was offered, my host had a friend from Bermuda on a visit. At the end of dinner he produced a beautiful cigarette case, and told us where it came from. My hearing was imperfect I leaned forward and said: "Did you say it came out of the Ark?" "Oh no it came from New Yark". I apologized humbly. The precious alpine flowers were in tins fading rapidly. Thursday night was spent in the train, sitting upright, swaying with the train, but with elbows pressed to the sides, drawing about 20 figures on thin scraps of paper, for tracing at the window pane on to the plates.

During these years at Haccombe and Coffinswell, and Milber it was usual for the Diocese to arrange a full series of visiting preachers for courses of instruction on week days in

Lent. This involved a lot of study, and the writer being
regarded as more free than most others, took such courses of
five sermons in each Lent at fifteen different churches, and in
more than one year at some of them, bicycling as far as
Chagford and Moreton. This was an addition to the work but
was happy and interesting. Looking back we realize that the
total of work fulfilled was only possible for a man in the prime
of life.

Astragalus alpinus

In both these years 1930–31 there was a further short trip
to the Clova mountains. In mid-July 1930 it was again by
the night train after seven services on the Sunday. There had
been a hot sunny June, and many alpine plants had gone to
seed early. One day Mr. Corstorphine kindly drove me to
Loch Rescobie near Forfar. We walked into a field where a
high wall supported a highland railway on our right. There
was a herd of highland cattle in the field. On the approach of
strangers they ran together, tail to tail, as they often do

with their long horns outwards, like a company with fixed
bayonets. But a young bull ran towards us with a loud
threatening growl, to dispute our passage. A quick council
of war decided that we were the farm boys. We walked on,
whistling or talking, with our sticks on our shoulders. And
the bull fortunately allowed us to pass. Indeed we were well
into the field, and there was no possible retreat except the
water of the loch. A local Pondweed (Pl. 90) and a *Lysimachia*
(Pl. 57) were safely gathered. There was a pretty little round
wasps' nest hanging from the underside of a horizontal willow
stem 5 yards out over the water very busy.

Thursday night was again spent making about 24 drawings
in the train, mostly of plants from the mountains, including
the beautiful lettuce *Cicerbita alpina* (Pl. 53). This night
travelling saved further hotel expense, and at least gave
freedom from interruption for drawing.

There were other little holidays with my wife and family,
but they were disappointingly short. Also after Sunday, 17
August 1930, the midnight train was again taken; I was in
Cambridge by 9.50 a.m. This time it was for the International
Botanical Congress which was held that year at Cambridge.
I could not afford the time or expense to join them in other
countries overseas. European countries were well represented
at Cambridge, also Americans, Indians and Japanese, etc. My
plates of that period were exhibited and commented upon.
The German botanists tried hard to persuade me to let them
go to Heidelberg for reproduction, but without success! We
must explain that this International Congress had a Nomen-
clature Committee, which during just the years of this century
were busy agreeing upon the international botanical names
of the species. Their final conclusions involved a lot of work
for me. One hundred and twenty of the old British names had
in later years to be washed out on the painted plates, and
replaced by international names.

We said that in 1930 many alpine plants in Scotland had
gone to seed by mid-July. So for 1931 my cousin William

Martin offered to accompany me to Clova with his car in the
middle of June, and we duly went, and my fellow clergy
undertook my Sunday duty. We visited Teesdale first and
arrived at Milton-of-Clova for a wet Sunday. We attended
the local Kirk, and the Minister was reading a lesson, most
impressively, e.g.: "He will destroy those murrderrers and
burrren up their city." We were kept in by stormy weather,
but at lunch-time on the 16th it lifted. We drove to the head
of the Glen and walked up Glen Dole to an eagle's eyrie. I
had to leave my cousin there as he was not fit to walk far,
and the main objective was the head of Caenlochan Glen some
four miles further on, but first we did a bit of snowballing,
and walked on solid bridges of snow over the burns. However, some two miles of South slope under Tom Buidhe was
clear of snow, and there were quantities of Loiseleuria, low
shrubby cushions, covered with little pink Azalea-like flowers.
And amongst these pretty cushions many pairs of ptarmigan
were nesting, some of the nests had three or four eggs. This
two-mile-long stretch of that South slope with no snow on it,
was an ideal place for the red deer to graze. And walking
quickly to the head of the glen towards Glas Maol round a
high upright rock I suddenly faced a big old stag with
immense antlers and many others behind him. What next?
Was it any use to raise my stick like the rifle I had handled
so often? We were within a few feet of one another. He
decided I was dangerous, and turned and led the great herd
down across the snow-clad glen, the line of deer stretching
right across it above the great wood, where we suppose they
spend the day. He was leading them to the South slope of
the next ridge in order to graze there. The rocks I wanted
to botanize on were under the snow. Hurrying back 7 miles
to the car and my companion in Glen Clova, I got to him
near 11 p.m. We returned via Teesdale to Coffinswell and
Milber.

✳ TORRINGTON

In the early spring of 1934 we were to leave the work at Coffinswell and Milber. The Dean and Chapter of Christ Church, Oxford had presented me to the Vicarage of Great Torrington, and just at this time candidates for Confirmation were being prepared at Milber. They were presented for Confirmation on 20 March, and they received their First Communion at 7.30 a.m. on the next morning. The Padre got down there on his bicycle early and he was instituted as Vicar of Great Torrington, North Devon, the same evening. And was at once very busy with Holy Week and Easter. There was no break in the work at all. And after Easter, the Rev. G. A. B. Jones, the assistant curate, left Torrington for High Bickington. So we were alone at the work there, as there was no adequate fund at all to maintain an assistant. We had a period of all-out work, visiting, preaching and teaching. The Vicarage house sadly needed modernizing. We found it needed most things, bathroom, modern sanitation, electricity, cooking facilities, so money had to be raised.

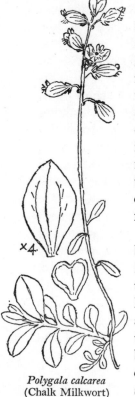

Polygala calcarea
(Chalk Milkwort)

The church bells were away at the foundry being re-cast. And they returned at the end of May, and were drawn through the streets by the schoolchildren. They were dedicated by Bishop Cecil in July. We took care to arrange a nice service, and the Bishop pulled off the tenor bell to the words of the blessing. The bells needed money too. So we got a finance committee appointed, and a free will offering scheme started. There was plenty of study

Papaver hybridum   *Hippocrepis comosa*

needed for the sermons, Bible classes, and teachers' preparations, and every house had to be visited. So there was little
time for any flower drawing. Recreation had to be obtained
in the big garden as we could not afford to keep the gardener.
Yet we had little outings to sisters in Exeter, and to the
South Devon coast. Times had changed. Very little domestic
help was possible. So my wife was busy. She was also working
up a large Mothers' Union branch, and a girls' Club. Without an assistant curate or with a deacon only, it was impossible
to go away for a holiday without kind help from other clergy.
But this help was given.

The holdays from Torrington were sometimes spent at
"St. Cross" in Streatham Drive, the home of my sisters in
Exeter, from which I could visit the museum collections of
flowers. These were studied with a view to the forthcoming

Flora of Devon. But also my cousin kindly took me for two nights to Lulworth Cove, bird watching in May. And while we were there the Chalk Milkwort (Pl. 11) *Papaver hybrida* (Pl. 5) and *Hippocrepis* (Pl. 24) were drawn.

In August that year, 1936, I was invited by my old school friend Oscar Watkins to visit Schloss Matsen, an old castle a few miles from Innsbruck in Austria. The castle belonged to Oscar's mother-in-law, an English lady who had married an Austrian. This was a wonderful old building partly of Roman Empire date. It had round towers with slits for archers. One big room was occupied with a large dining-table all laid ready for a meal in medieval style, with pewter plates and drinking vessels, and chairs all of old cross-legged pattern. There was a wide moat outside, which produced a crowd of mosquitoes. I killed 24 on my friend's back one day. He drove me into Bavaria to a Passion play. And another day we walked up to the snow line, probably 7,000 feet on some peak. There, just at the edge of the snow, we lifted tiny seedling plants of Soldanella, Gentian and the yellow *Viola biflora*. These and others passed through the customs and were planted on a new rockery at Torrington, where they flowered nicely. But in the war we kept geese, and they got out and found the plants and said "Here is something new", and they ate them all right down to the roots.

But in referring to the war we are anticipating. In one of these winters in the very coldest weather, a serious tragedy occurred in Torrington. Sydney House, a very large house in South Street, was taken over by the Devon County Council as a boarding school for backward boys. I went there with some regularity for little services of instruction. And I left there my old army knapsack, full of hymn books. One evening when the boys were all in bed, the staff were having supper together. But one of them had been ironing, and had left an electric iron switched on in the ironing-room. The house had been constructed with a large central hall open right up to the roof with broad and beautiful oak staircases,

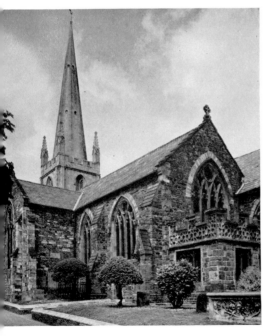

St. Luke's Church, Milber, near Newton Abbot; its design was revealed to the author in a dream. See page 105 for plan of the interior

Torrington Parish Church where the author was Vicar from 1934 to 1943

The Rev. W. Keble Martin in 1960

After the wedding at
Powderham Church on
27 January 1965

Flora Martin after the wedding; with her brother, Arthur
Stidston, who gave her away

After receiving an Honorary Degree of Doctor of Science at Exeter University 30 June, 1966. With Professor C. F. Parker, Professor R. Niklaus, Mr. K. C. H. Rowe, Pro Chancellor, and Her Grace Mary Duchess of Devonshire, Chancellor of Exeter University

and galleries for access to the bedrooms. This proved a most dangerous construction. Presently smoke was pouring out from the door of the ironing-room, immediately poisoning the atmosphere of all the stairs and galleries. Boys began coming down and at first were sent back by a teacher, not realizing the seriousness of the situation. By the time the fire-brigade arrived the situation was desperate. Most of the boys were got down, all but seven. Some of these had dived under their beds to get air. Bill Kelly (our good church verger) was the captain of the fire-brigade. He entered top-floor windows at great risk from a fire escape, and brought down four or five boys, but all seven died of carbon monoxide poisoning. The ruins of the building were a mass of great icicles in the morning. And in due course we had a truly sad funeral gathering. One lesson from this occasion seems to be that even if there is a small fire, where children are concerned, the first thing to be done is to get the children outside.

In another year (1937), my wife went for a visit to her friends as the family were already dispersed, and my cousin Willy Martin took me in his car to Lydford, west of Dartmoor. And we walked up to Great Links Tor (1,900 feet). There were tiny plants of a common meadow buttercup only an inch high below the rocks. But from Links Tor we saw what appeared to be a chalk pit some three miles to the west of us. This was most unexpected. The snow-white pit or quarry was on Burley Down, a ridge about three miles long. So from Lydford we were off the next morning to visit Burley Down. Geologists would know all about it, but it was new to us. The plants around the edge of the white pit were heather and other non-calcareous kinds. A short distance from the white powder the rock strata were obviously not horizontal but vertical, standing on edge, with very smoky surfaces between them. A few feet further away still the rock was quite unburnt. So we sent samples to the Geological Institute in London. The rock was radiolarian chert, deeply burnt in part by the white-hot granite, and then rolled off

Dartmoor, probably by a further rise of the granite. The white powder is the burnt rock, and is the pot clay used for the Devon pottery, teapots, and kitchen sinks, etc. Most of it has been washed away to sea, but there are beds of it in hollows, one at Peters Marland in North Devon, two miles long, and another from Bovey Tracey to Newton Abbot in South Devon, five or six miles long. Rocks falling even on a mountain face make a very loud noise, but can you imagine a mass three miles long and 200 feet high rolling, smoking off the white-hot granite? Now curlews nest peacefully on Burley Down.

Empetrum nigrum

✳ THE FLORA OF DEVON

The next few days of this holiday were spent searching wide areas of central Dartmoor with G. T. Fraser and other botanists, and a drawing of Empetrum (Pl. 55) was made. We also went to some wooded valleys, such as Lydford Gorge and Fingle. It was a small part of the preparation for issuing a *Flora of Devon*. This was quite a serious big work of 750 pages, promoted by the Devonshire Association. There were several meetings of the editorial committee of five members with Mr. G. F. Tregelles, chairman, and Mr. F. A. Brokenshire, secretary. Seven botanists contributed studies of the flora of particular areas. We cannot refrain from mentioning the masterly account of Braunton Burrows by Dr. F. R. Ellison-Wright. It seemed to fall to the Vicar of Torrington to be the principal editor, but he was helped by Mr. G. T. Fraser. Quite a lot of evening work had to be put into it, but it brought us in contact with another group of our fellow men. Fortunately it was peace-time, and there was an assistant curate, the Rev. H. S. Rhodes. The *Flora of Devon* was published by Buncle & Co. just before the last war, 1939, and paper was already restricted. Only 500 copies were printed. They are rare, and people sometimes advertise their need of a copy.

But to complete the holiday referred to above, a trip was made with my wife by train to Derby, to her old home at Ashbourne and Dove Dale, and even to my first parish of Wath-on-Dearne, where we met some good old friends after 16 years' absence. And so back by train to Torrington. We wrote a happy letter about this holiday in the August Parish Magazine. This was exceptional, because it was always our aim to send a church message.

In Torrington we were busy again. Some people seem to think that a padre can preach a sermon just out of his head. We are not so clever. It is necessary to spend a lot of time

in study, to learn all about the subject in order to make
sermons and class teaching really instructive. I have never
preached another man's sermon. Much weakness of faith today is surely due to people not knowing what has been the
deep experience of mankind in the past, recorded in the
Scriptures, and so what may indeed be our own moving experience today, a personal loyalty, which we check up on at
the end of each day by self examination.

There was always a full week's work at Torrington and
nothing unusual in it, visiting, teaching and meetings.
Recreation still mostly in the garden. Sometimes a walk on
the Commons with my wife. There were Grasshopper
warblers singing there in summer and beautiful flowers in
the marshes.

Bishop Cecil of Exeter had passed on and Charles Edward
Curzon had become our Bishop in October 1936.

✳ 1938

We were really very fortunate in having so much help from
kind friends to take us out. In the following January we were
given a lift, and we led our friends to the rock on which the
tiny fern *Asplenium septentrionale* still grows. We found it in
good condition, showing no likelihood of dying out. This is
in the southern half of Devon; there is a little of it on the
North Devon coast too. The name *septentrionale* means
northern. It is a plant of sub-arctic regions. And discussing
it with Mr. Wilmot, who was then the head botanist at the
British Museum (Natural History), he remarked that its
existence in Devon is a proof that the climate there was once
of a more arctic type. It is becoming warmer. So in winter
that is encouraging.

There followed some months of busy parochial work. We have tried to be "a workman that needeth not to be ashamed". And then on 23 May, we went off to attend the 150th Anniversary of the Linnean Society in London. I did sometimes— attend the ordinary meetings at Burlington House and exhibited drawings at them. But this anniversary gathering was held in Albemarle Street for more accommodation. So we wrote in the June Parish Magazine: "It has been the writer's privilege this week to attend a long series of addresses describing some of the latest discoveries and conclusions of a dozen of the greatest biologists of Europe, drawn from nine different countries. If some of our members fancy that modern science is not compatible with the Christian faith, it may be of some help to them to be assured that this is not at all the case." These two aspects of truth complete one another. We speak of natural law, let us call it the trustworthiness of nature, mercifully provided for us.

Yet of all the meetings and discussions there was one thing which stuck in my mind. A learned professor delivering a discourse on his own subject, seemed to digress in order to pour scorn on the Creation picture in the Book of Genesis in the first chapter of the Bible. There was no opportunity of replying. But we felt that if he had studied what he was referring to, he would have realized that Abraham merely pictures the Babylonian tradition current at that time, and now well known from contemporary inscriptions. But Abraham reproduced it with one great difference, namely that its gross heathen character is removed. And the Creation is pictured as the work of one Creator, who is entirely good, a wonderful inspiration. And great emphasis is laid on the truth that every aspect of creation is good and beautiful, not evil as others said, and also that man has a small share of likeness with the Creator, namely personality, responsible, with understanding enough to progressively know and subdue nature. The professor apparently expected Abraham to forestall the knowledge given us today.

Immediately after this gathering, my holiday was completed by being taken to Padstow and Pentire Head in Cornwall for bird watching. There were seals sunning themselves on the beach, but we were chiefly interested in the numerous choughs on the cliffs with their red beaks and legs. On the top of this headland, suitable to its name, we picked up a complete and very good fountain pen, which we lodged with the police at Wadebridge, and it came back to us a year later unclaimed.

And so back to the busy round of work for a parochial flock, which did seem to need all our efforts. We usually had a garden fête at the Vicarage at about the end of July, for which a working party made lengthy preparation. The fête was a good social occasion, and made a useful contribution to funds.

At least two of these fête days were very wet. On one occasion the rain began shortly before the opening and we carried all the stalls into the Vicarage house with plenty of wet mud from the garden. Some lady pointing to the mud remarked: "I am glad I am not the Vicar's wife." My wife overheard it and was murmuring "I am sure he is too". I hope the first lady did not hear the quick response.

As Christmas approached that year my assistant curate, the Rev. Harold Rhodes, prepared a Nativity play and trained a lot of members for their parts. He did it very well. The play was presented in the nave of the church, in front of the screen. It was quite a good experience for those who took part, and attracted an attendance of about 500. My friend, Mr. G. B. Blatchford, the churchwarden, sang the Nunc Dimittis with real feeling.

About this time some nasty things were said about the Vicar, especially over the restoration of a penitent member to Communion. But he has nothing to regret, and he hopes that those who said these things were sorry later on. About the same time he was encouraged by a small compliment. A man who disagreed with him over a little matter said: "We know that you are a worker, but I cannot agree over this."

We belong to a wonderful society. And we need to be very careful not to say nasty things about those around us. Referring back to my first parish, and the beginning of the First World War, we will call them X, Y and Z. X in a private conversation suggested Y for some trusted duty. I objected, saying: "I am afraid he is apt to do so and so that is wrong." Soon afterwards I had convincing evidence that this was quite untrue. It was merely jealous slander. I went back to X and apologized for having said it. But X had already repeated it to Z and others. Slander is always like a snowball. I had learned a lesson. If we witness Y doing wrong, we can speak our mind to Y, but with wisdom. It is a great help to some of us to have a trusted bosom friend, with whom we can talk things over, and who can correct us or point out our omissions. I am all in favour of wisely married clergy. But make quite sure that the lady will be a help meet for you!

One last item before the war began: after the fête in 1939 we managed to take our family away for a holiday on Exmoor. We all stayed at the Warren Farm near the head of the Exe in Simonsbath. We had nice walks in sunny weather on the tops and in the Exe and Doone valleys. We enjoyed the moorland birds, and seeing the red deer lying in the bracken for concealment. One evening a dozen of these came into the garden at dusk to eat the cabbages. We had the pleasure of finding quite a lot of the little Orchid *Listera cordata* (Pl. 80) which had been supposed not to grow in Devon.

Circumstances changed with the beginning of the war, and were similar to those of many other places. There was a good drill hall, so we were soon billeted with a battalion. The Vicarage had one officer and six other ranks. The house was full. And there followed a steady stream of children from the London area. The billeting officer seemed to have to refer continually to the Vicar and his wife for help. We seemed to have more knowledge of the local families and households. So my wife was busy helping with this.

We also had a group of weddings, and one of these was

the wedding of my own youngest daughter Lisette who, on
7 October, married John Asa Whitney, who had been all over
the world in sailing ships, and was now in the Royal Naval
Reserve, and was to do later some specially useful work on
Normandy beaches. Of the rest of my family, my son Patrick
was now working for the Assam Tea Company in India. And
he was called up for military training at Bangalore, from
which he was later sent to South Africa. My daughter
Barbara, a physical training teacher for the Devon County
Council, was presently posted to Taunton Hospital, and later
to Windsor Hospital. My daughter Vivienne went into the
Auxiliary Transport Service, and became busy driving.

The parochial work at Torrington continued at full pressure, but in the following May my fellow worker, Harold
Rhodes, was called away to a curacy at Paignton. Our population had much increased. I was distressed at the difficulty
of maintaining a high standard of parochial work. I paid eight
visits to theological colleges looking for a deacon. But at last
we secured the help of the Rev. B. S. Crockett, who came in
September from a curacy at Ottery St. Mary. And the work
went on duly shared. It was impossible to hold a garden fête.
So we had a gift day instead. All the proceeds of several
working parties were being sent to men in the forces, to
Torrington men, to Devon regiments, to minesweepers, and
to the Merchant Navy. We published frequently full lists of
Torrington men serving in the forces, to enable us to think
of them.

One small item of this period comes to mind. Before the
war, the Rector and two church members from Torrington
in Connecticut, U.S.A., had called on us, and explained that
there is a Society of St. George there to keep the younger
members in contact with the best English ideals. They have
also a foundation stone from Torrington, Devon. And when
the war had been on for a year, there was happy contact with
them again. They contributed an ambulance duly inscribed
and presented to Torrington, Devon. This was to be used

wherever it was thought best. And we had a nice letter saying: "Our thoughts and prayers are very much with you in these days."

We have omitted to say that we had started a Church Youth Fellowship in Torrington. And just before the war we were building a Church House. This had one classroom and a kitchen downstairs and a larger room upstairs. It was designed by my brother. And although, owing to the war, it was rather incomplete, this building was opened and dedicated at the Harvest Thanksgiving (1940). The lower room was at once adapted as a writing and recreation room for members of H.M. forces. The large upper room was used for the senior Sunday School and church meetings, and also for a Sunday breakfast party once a month. This last was held after the 8 a.m. service. And the Church Youth Fellowship provided this breakfast, with all the crockery required, and even the food out of their own rations. They did all the work involved, and it proved a very happy gathering of about two dozen members. It helped us to mix and to know one another.

There was another item almost completed before the war. This was the south chapel of the Parish Church. It had been provided with a nice carved screen (the work of Mr. Herbert Read of Exeter), and with suitable furnishings in memory of my predecessor, Archdeacon Emlyn Jones. And this was dedicated at the same Harvest Thanksgiving. And we found it very convenient for everyday services.

We have, as may be expected, no record of holidays or of flower painting in this period. We had very continuous work. There was indeed a pouring out of the soul in visiting and in Christian messages of encouragement. One side of the work that received special attention was the effort to win younger members. A Youth Week-end Conference was held for which the Diocesan Missioner came. A United Youth Council was formed for all the churches in the town. A United Sunday School Teacher's gathering was held in the Church House, attended by 36 teachers, a number soon much reduced by the

"Call-up". The children's Sunday worship at 10 a.m. was improved, parents attending and receiving Communion at it once a month in presence of their children. Our own Church Youth Fellowship helped in leadership to evacuee children, many of them now from Bristol.

Otherwise, the work was the same kind of picture as in most other parishes, Red Cross working parties and much Blood Transfusion to help the wounded, together with more than normal teaching and worship. Meanwhile the Rev. B. S. Crockett left us and became Vicar of a Somerset parish in September 1941. And the writer, as Vicar of Torrington, was alone in his parish work all the following winter, and he was also Rural Dean, visiting other churches by walking and bicycling. My wife was doing splendid work at the British Restaurant. She was clever at choosing workers, and forceful in persuading them to do it.

About the beginning of May 1942, Exeter was badly bombed, and the Cathedral was severely damaged, so our intercessions and offerings at early services were devoted to Exeter churches. But in the early spring we had been given the expectation of help. Edward Eliot, an ex-ship's captain, training at Wells Theological College, was to be ordained deacon for work in Torrington. Owing to damage at the Cathedral, his ordination was at Crediton on Trinity Sunday, 31 May. This was a great encouragement, for we were pretty well tired out. He and his wife came at the beginning of June.

Unfortunately when Mr. Eliot had been with us for only six weeks, the Vicar, who had overworked a bit, was suddenly incapacitated by severe sciatica, while visiting the hospital. I was unavoidably out of action for three weeks and had to be entrusted to the care of the Sisters of St. Francis at Posbury near Crediton. I soon recovered with rest and their great kindness, and returned to Torrington. And with Mr. Eliot, some of the visiting was done in co-operation. In the autumn, our former schoolmaster was seriously ill. He had the reputation of having been severe, he was feared by little boys. One day when I called he said to me: "We are all God's little children after all." He died a few weeks later.

On the first Sunday in Lent the following year (1943) Bishop Curzon of Exeter held his ordination in Torrington Church, so it fell to my lot to prepare for this service. Edward Eliot was ordained priest. This was a great and happy occasion for us all. The Bishop was in fact rather enthusiastic about the church work at Torrington.

But just at this time there came an important decision for me. The approaching Eastertide would be my tenth in Torrington. And during the last three and a half years, the work had been very exacting. And there had not been enough quiet time for study. In consequence I had to preach almost in the words of sermons which I had preached there already. And so I felt very strongly that I had delivered my message in Torrington. About this time the Rector of Combe-in-Teignhead with Milber (the Rev. J. Timms) was appointed Vicar of Buckfastleigh. And messages came to me that some people at Milber were saying: "We cannot build the houses, and we cannot build the Church. That Martin started the Church here, and the Church will never be needed." And I felt very responsible for having started it.

Sir Bourchier Wrey offered me the benefice of Combe-in-Teignhead with Milber. And I thought I ought to go and bear the brunt of the supposed difficulties. I was very confident that the Dean and Chapter of Christ Church in Oxford, who were the patrons of Torrington, would find a suitable man to carry on there with a fresh message. It happened that the Dean was Dr. Lowe, who had come from Canada. He came to Torrington and interviewed the churchwardens, without me! The Bishop of Exeter tried to get their nominee for the appointment changed but without success. And the blame fell on me for leaving the place.

*　*　*

* NATURE PRESERVATION

At the end of our stay at Torrington I was very anxious to help in the preservation of places of natural beauty and interest. I found I could attend meetings for this purpose more easily from Combe-in-Teignhead. I therefore attended all the eight meetings of the "Nature Reserves Investigation Committee" (Sub-Committee for Devon). These were long meetings, morning and afternoon, held at Mardon Hall of the University College of Exeter, under the able chairmanship of Professor L. A. Harvey from December 1942 to January 1944. We were usually seven members and we had each of us submitted a memorandum at the first meeting. The members of this sub-committee were Professor L. A. Harvey (chairman and convener), Mr. D. St. Leger-Gordon (Dartmoor), Mr. H. McClelland (Forestry), Mr. F. Horne (Agriculture), Mr. F. C. Butters (Birds), Mr. L. N. Staniland (Insects), W.K.M. (Botany), also Mr. R. Handsford-Worth submitted a memorandum on the Archaeology. My own was the longest and referred to some 30 areas of Devon.

Professor Harvey gave us at each meeting full typed copies of the business of the previous meeting. And one joint meeting with the Somerset Sub-Committee was held at Taunton with reference to Exmoor. These discussions were deeply interesting regarding the moors, the woodlands, the coastal areas, and the general amenities offered by Devon to visitors from other parts. On one of these days in the war we could not easily find any luncheon in Exeter, till at last we landed amongst another community of fellow men at the Ship Inn in St. Martin's Lane, on wooden benches with an inch-thick sandwich and a tankard of beer.

This Investigation Committee recommended that two large moorland areas should become National Parks (and agreed on their boundaries) that three areas should be National Reserves, and four smaller ones Local reserves, also seven areas Amenity reserves. In December 1944, as a further result of these meetings, Professor Harvey drew up proposals for a South West Naturalist Trust or Union. And I had afterwards the pleasure of walking over some questionable areas like Haldon Hills with Professor Harvey. But I have not attended meetings since. It was very difficult for me to travel to them. I felt it was for younger men to carry on. But we trust that the work of this Nature Reserves Investigation Committee laid a useful foundation for future work on the same lines. When I could travel I wanted to go to Kew or the Natural History Museum; but not yet. No flower drawing was done during the war.

When we left Torrington for Combe and Milber some people thought it was unwise of us to go back to the Milber work. But I had never been the responsible Vicar of that area, only a voluntary curate, and now I was to be Vicar and to bear the brunt of any alleged difficulties. It was our intention to get on with the visiting, and application was made at once for a permit for an autocycle. We had to wait seven months for it. But when it came it was a great help. It went up those two steep hills at the same pace as it went down, and carried the Vicar often three times a day to and fro for visitings and meetings.

There was steady progress in the raising of funds for church building at Milber, and the numbers of the confirmation candidates were maintained. My wife worked very happily with others in the sewing parties at Milber. In the first autumn, 1943, she opened their bazaar, and was a great help with these workers in the years that followed; and also with the Mothers' Union. In her I had a valuable helper. While the war lasted there were the usual difficulties. It was all-out work. No service after dark at Combe owing to the blackout. No organist at Combe owing to military service. Mr. Butler came for a while, then Mr. A. E. Godfrey, a lawyer's clerk at Newton Abbot, took on the organ. He stuck at it and was an immense help and in 1968 he is still the

organist there. Mr. C. H. Johnson, the lay reader, left and
in June 1945, at the end of the war, Mr. Penry Thomas was
admitted as lay reader, and he proved a most valuable helper,
most often taking one of the two evensong services. So the
work went on for six years.

As soon as the war was over we started little outings. In
July 1945, my wife and I went to Newbridge on the Dart,
and *Sibthorpia* (Pl. 63) and its flower enlargement were
drawn; another day to Landscove for a mullein. And at the
end of July, I went with my cousin Willy Martin on a brief
visit to Teesdale, staying with Dr. Murphy at Whistle Crag,
a very windy spot. *Lysimachia ciliata* (Pl. 57) and *Serratula*
(Pl. 49) were drawn. In November my wife and I went to
Berry Head and *Solanum nigrum* was added, and two local
Milber plants were drawn. But the parochial work was kept
up.

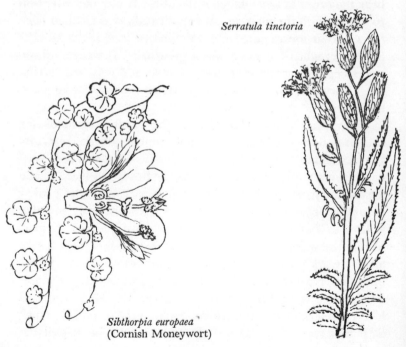

Serratula tinctoria

Sibthorpia europaea
(Cornish Moneywort)

During this period the church accommodation at Milber consisted of the Lady Chapel permanently built with a considerable wooden extension for temporary seating. And at Easter 1946, when some had returned from the forces, this accomodation was stretched to the uttermost for the early Communion. I took the 7.30 a.m. at Combe and another priest took the 8.30 a.m. at Milber, in case I should be late. When I arrived there ready robed, I could hardly squeeze in at the door to kneel on the doormat, till it was time to go up and assist. Standing room was filled to bursting. There did not appear to be any serious falling off owing to the same padre coming back to the work. But one thing that clergy do not know is exactly where or how far their witness and work has been effective.

In the remaining years at Combe after the war we were restricted by financial difficulties like many others and we hardly went for any expeditions. And the flower drawing did not advance. We were very busy with the parochial work. Yet in June 1948, I was given a lovely brief trip to Dinnet near Balmoral in Aberdeenshire, where my youngest daughter Lisette Whitney and her husband were staying with their two children. And they kindly gave me a lift, as far as roads permitted, in order that I might walk to Lochnagar to botanize on the high rocks above the loch. It was beautiful, but I was alone facing the elements, climbing about at 3,700 feet at age 71. They waited patiently for me to return. *Alchemilla glabra* (Pl. 26) from a meadow near Dinnet was the only plant drawn.

Early in 1947 a few weeks of serious snow had made the steep hills almost impassable. I mostly walked, but when I went to the expense of a taxi home, the driver refused to go down into Combe, saying he would never get up again. At other times in fog the auto-bike travelling was terribly cold. Worse than that a large area beside the hill from Milber was built up. There were always people on the road after dark, and my machine was lighted off the engine. Uphill the light went dim, and I was in serious danger of knocking people down, I said it must stop. I could not risk this for another winter season. I was asking for some parish with less difficult travelling; but there seemed to be no prospect of being offered one. So I was compelled to resign from my benefice in 1949 at age 72.

We were preparing a small bungalow with the help of my cousin Willy Martin (of Longcause, Dartington). The bungalow was at Gidleigh on the north-east edge of Dartmoor, three miles from Chagford. We had to buy a small and rather boggy field called on the tithe map "Broadymead". It had some old oak trees with buzzards nesting in them, and a sub-moorland flora. A little stream soon bridged, separated us from a wood. The woodland birds included two pairs of Greater Spotted woodpeckers. We had kind neighbouring farmers on both sides, and went daily for milk to one of them. We moved in at the end of the summer of 1949. And soon began to make rapid progress with drawing flowers. Several bog loving grasses and sedges were added from our own field.

I had resigned from my benefice, that is from my office as Vicar; but no man ordained a priest can possibly resign from his priesthood. The rules of the Church are hard on those who resign their vicariate. They must live in a parish somewhere; but they are not allowed to be on the electoral roll of the parish or to have any voice or share in its Parochial Church meetings. The Rector of Gidleigh, the Rev. Townsell was very kind and allowed me to be in his choir and to read the lessons sometimes at mattins or evensong but something more important also happened.

When we moved to Gidleigh near Chagford, I was put on a list called "Special Service Clergy", and was posted by its secretary to any parish needing help. And when I had done some 30 week-ends of services and visiting, I was licensed in the Cathedral by Bishop Robert Mortimer as a Public Preacher.

But in the early part of this period, other works were interrupted by the illness and death of my friend and cousin Willy
Martin. He had stayed with us when we first got to Gidleigh.
Now there were several visits to him in hospital, then fulfil-
ling the last offices at Dartington. After that there were no
less than eight visits to "Longcause", Dartington, to clear
up his affairs as his executor. The dear man always put letters
and legal documents back into the envelopes they arrived in,
and filed nothing. So hundreds of envelopes had to be opened.
He had been on night duty through the war as a warden.
And he had been a great help to me, taking me out each
springtime since the war, for a day or two on some coast,
and even coming with me to Teesdale and the Clova Mountains.

In the spring of 1950, I had the opportunity of attending
a meeting of the Linnean Society and also of exhibiting at a
Botanical Society meeting. Then we visited my daughter
Barbara at Windsor. She was working at Windsor Hospital
and we attended services at St. George's Chapel. My cousin
Sir Walter Moberly was Librarian at Windsor Castle at that
time.

At midsummer 1952, my wife and I went on a long and
wonderful holiday, meeting many old friends. We were away
for 20 days including three Sundays. First we visited my
sisters in Exeter, and then we went by train and bus to Derby
and Ashbourne. We had a Sunday at Ashbourne Church,
where I had been a curate, and my wife a regular worshipper,
and where we were married more than 40 years previously.
Dr. Hollick (see page 64) was still there, married and with a
grown up daughter. We had tea with them and discussed
the flower drawings. We even stayed two nights at the Isaac
Walton Hotel in Dove Dale, and visited old haunts, Thorpe
Cloud and Bunster, and walked down the Dale from Dove
Holes to the Stepping Stones. The drawing of *Eleocharis
palustris* (Pl. 91) came from this walk.

From Ashbourne and Derby we went by train to Edinburgh

5

and Killin Junction. There the expected train from Oban had
not arrived. It was late. We asked how long it would be and
met the answer: "a wee while." We timed the "wee while"
and found it 43 minutes. They did not seem to be in a hurry
in Scotland. We arrived at Ben Lawers Hotel. We attended
the Kirk on Sunday, and explored the walk to the Lawers
burn. We received kind help and guidance from Mr. Stelfox
of Dublin. On Monday, two days before my 75th birthday,
we walked together up the burn. But at 2 p.m. I soon had to
leave my wife to return to the hotel, while I went on up past
the Lochan to the top and gathered alpine plants, as directed
by Mr. Stelfox.

I had promised to start back at 5 o'clock, to be back in
time for dinner. I was alone on the top admiring some little
mountain woodrushes when suddenly we were wrapped in
dense mist; in a minute drenching rain began and a severe
thunderstorm burst. The lightning was much branched, striking the ground all around. A wonderful sight, it was a noisy
bombardment, quite continuous. This lasted for what seemed
many minutes, while I walked quickly eastwards in dense
mist and then ran down. There were waterfalls everywhere.
When I had gone down 2,000 feet the sun came out and
seemed to be going down in the east! This was Glen Lyon
on the wrong side. I wanted to say: "I am all right but shall
be very late." It took two hours to get up again, then I went
on round the top till I saw Loch Tay, and ran down in another
storm by about 10.30. I am afraid some had started out to
look for me, but fortunately were driven back by the mist
and the second storm. Two days later we had a long walk
together in the Taymouth Castle area.

Soon after this we returned by train to Yorkshire and
visited Wath-on-Dearne. I had been vicar there for 13 years
but had left 31 years since (p. 72–87). Dr. Adam Johnston was
still there and was most hospitable to us, and drove us around
by Wentworth and later to Sheffield. On the Sunday Mr.
Evans the Vicar kindly allowed me to take the 8 a.m. Holy

Communion service there and to preach at 11 a.m. Our friend Millington the verger was still there amongst the others. It has often been our joy to meet old friends in this way, friends still here in this short pilgrimage.

The last two days of this holiday were spent in London, comparing and drawing flowers at the Natural History Museum and meeting some of our expert botanists, a fitting end to a great holiday.

After this, ten week-ends from Gidleigh were spent at Lew Trenchard, staying usually in the house which had been the home of S. Baring Gould, author of some hymns (Onward Christian Soldiers, etc.). He had been vicar there for 49 years. This week-end plan was now taking a definite shape. It became my rule to arrive at a lodging in time for luncheon on Saturday, to spend that afternoon and evening visiting all the time, and also Sunday afternoon. That is to say I was visiting, just when the men were more likely to be at home, sometimes they were gardening. I received encouragement in this work from Bishop Cockin of Bristol, whom I met at tea with my sisters in Exeter. I not only released a number of clergy for holidays or during sickness, working in about 46 different churches, but filled also the gap between one vicar and the next, in seven parishes, including Lew Trenchard 11 weeks, South Taunton 24 weeks, Spreyton 30 weeks, Drewsteignton 32 weeks, Belston 9 weeks, Moretonhampstead 6 weeks. I was duly sent to Moreton for the whole vacancy but I found another priest living in the parish, and he wanted to do the work in the parish, so I handed it to him. This was in addition to taking the duty at Gidleigh (where we lived) for about 14 months during the Rector's illness and after his death.

The auto-cycle used at Milber proved unsuitable and the car had to be maintained. There was an allowance of 6d. per mile for travelling. And the Sunday services were paid for at a guinea a service, as at the end of last century, when we irreverently called stop-gap clergy guinea-pigs. The visiting was voluntary work, just as it had been in early days at

Milber. Its own reward, you may say, for we have enjoyed and still enjoy the privilege of talking sincerely to our fellow-men, and sharing with them the joy of the Christian life.

During these years at Gidleigh, when the writer no longer held a benefice, he was usually in charge of a parish during the winter months in five successive years; but he had more scattered engagements in the summer. And the work of flower drawing advanced rapidly. And spare time was given to it, also 20 plates were retraced and repainted, adjusting the spacing of figures to make them more even. Some 200 specimens were received by post from other botanists. These were a great help, sometimes for the improvement of a figure, but often for first drawing. A few visits were also made to two brothers who lived in Surrey, and then to the Natural History Museum in London and to the Kew Herbarium. This was most valuable for comparison of specimens and for adding those which could not be obtained. Members of the staff in each case were most helpful.

In August 1957, soon after my 80th birthday, I had to go to the Devon and Exeter Hospital for a common but serious operation, followed by a few weeks at a Moreton Hampstead Nursing Home, and my activities were curtailed for a while, though I soon got back to a bit of gardening. One of the most serious difficulties of our life at Gidleigh was that the church at half a mile away was some 200 feet above us. We needed, in our advancing age, to be able to walk into the local church easily, not puffing and blowing.

We visited a number of villages in search of a more favourably placed bungalow, but we did not find one. So in one of these we took steps to purchase a site and to build one. The price of the site and the character of the bungalow were agreed with the land owner, with the help of our lawyers, who drew out a plan of the site. But it appeared that the patron of the benefice had some rights regarding it. And he objected to a small house being built near the church. So we went ourselves to ask his consent. "No! You may be a very nice man, but you will very soon be dead, and your successor may be a horrid man." But the speaker himself was the one who did not live long after saying this.

✳ WOODBURY

After touring all around we came to Woodbury, where the Devon Contractors were building bungalows, and first we chose a site on the Summerfield estate. But then hearing of their intention to build in Pound Lane, we chose the site there that was nearest to the church. It was after visiting Woodbury in November 1957 that my wife had her first stroke. Our neighbours at Gidleigh were very kind indeed at that time, but I was now much tied at home. The Gidleigh bungalow was sold for us. And we had an expensive homeless time with furniture in store. We got the standard bungalow design of the Devon Contractors adapted a little, giving a big south window to the kitchen, making this into a little square breakfast-room. The sitting-room was also made brighter by opening into a little greenhouse on the south. We took the name Broadymead with us, and moved into this Woodbury bungalow early in March 1958.

Soon after this I was asked to take charge of Clyst St. George Church during the vacancy caused by Mr. Bray, the Vicar, going to Australia. I accepted this duty but it was two miles away and I had no car. I went by bus to the visiting, especially on Saturday afternoons, but on other days too. And I was carried to and fro by voluntary drivers to attend the services on Sundays at 8 a.m., 11 a.m., and 6.30 p.m. In fact this voluntary transport made the two-mile journey six times every Sunday, or some 360 times in all, and never failed once, a wonderful achievement. But behind it was Mr. Drury, churchwarden (the Cathedral architect). He organized it. If nobody else could do it, he did it himself. I had the happiness of meeting fellow church members both on these lifts and in the visiting by bus on weekdays. The visiting and the Confirmation Classes and Sick Communions were as usual voluntary or unpaid work. Perhaps that was one of the facts which made this again a truly happy period. It lasted for 58 weeks.

The period of duty at Clyst St. George ended with the institution of a new rector on 6 July, 1959. And two days later we celebrated our golden wedding, 8 July. We had a full family gathering and we were given some beautiful glass-ware decorated with gold. We had completed 50 years of married life together. We had co-operated happily. And as we recalled our activities together in the earlier years, we realized that we had wonderful blessings to be thankful for. Barbara had come overnight from her work at Bedford Physical Training College. She, poor dear, already knew that she was suffering from leukaemia but did not tell us owing to her mother's frail health.

In the previous January my coloured drawings of British Flowers had been exhibited at the Royal Horticultural Society Meeting in Vincent Square. That was when the Hon. Sir David Bowes-Lyon was president, and later on he was one of those who signed an appeal for their publication. And after the work at Clyst St. George was over, there followed a period of more occasional church duty. And during this time the work of drawing the flowers went on steadily; we were also trying in vain to get some publisher to reproduce them.

The year 1960 was a sad year for the family. On Sunday, 6 March, their mother had a severe heart attack. The doctor and the parish nurse were in the house daily that week. And although she gradually recovered, she was from that date more dependent on the help of others. However, I was still able to be occupied with some church work, taking, in that spring and summer, several Sundays at different churches.

On 16 June our family doctor came and told us that our dear eldest daughter, Barbara, was really desperately ill with leukaemia, that she probably had only a few months to live. She was at the Radcliff Infirmary at Oxford. And I was soon taken to see her there. Barbara had known for 18 months, but had kept it from us, because her mother was ill. Though we could see that she had become anaemic. For more than half the period she had kept on her good work at Bedford Physical Training College, but had now given it up. So we were visiting her, first at Oxford, then almost daily at the Devon and Exeter Hospital, and finally at Mellands in Powderham, the home of our youngest daughter Lisette Whitney.

Barbara had been a good intimate friend, a very dear eldest daughter. She had been engaged in the training of teachers in remedial work for children, and also latterly we believe running a clinic at the College. She often attended hospital courses during vacations, and her work was undoubtedly blest. Her hobby was bird watching, as she was a good ornithologist. She was at the last completely resigned to her call. She quoted a prayer of one Philip Neri, which said: "God's will for me is always better than my own will." As I told her, I longed to change places with her, but it was not to be. She died at Mellands in Powderham on 12 November 1960, aged 48. At a Memorial Service at St. Mary's, Bedford, there were more than a hundred communicants. We gathered that Barbara had helped to win others to church worship.

During this same period our little home in Pound Lane, Woodbury, was in danger from a flood. A heavy "cloud burst" on Woodbury Common amounting to $3\frac{1}{2}$ inches of rain, flooded the little brook, which passes in a deep bed close behind the house. It also flooded the sewers with surface water. We were at the end of a branch sewer. Three manhole lids were lifted, and the water poured out over the garden.

It was the forenoon of 30 September. I went into the kitchen
to speak to a woman, who was giving us valuable help at the
time. And at that moment we saw an alarming sight close
outside the window. The earth opened at the edge of the
lawn. The herbaceous border in full autumn flower went away
to the left into the bed of the stream, carrying a rose pergola
and wooden fence with it, leaving a little cliff some 10 feet
high which extended within a few feet of the back door, in
fact under the flagstone there. Help was urgently called for
from the Devon Contractors who built the bungalow. They
promptly took men, we believe, from other work, and we
were very grateful. They shored it up; and then built a re-
inforced concrete wall to the brook and tipped in a contribution
of 65 tons of soil behind it, and refixed the fence. It cost £350.
But Ecclesiastical Insurance contributed half of it, as an act
of grace, although their policy did not cover flood damage.
We also received a kind gift, passed on by the Bishop of
Exeter from the Church of St. James, West Derby, Liverpool, of £12.

Lower down the same stream at Exton, the old church
building of cob and thatch was surrounded with flood water.
As a building it had stood apparently for 400 years. But now
the cob walls melted in the flood water, and the thatched roof
was let down. But many of the fittings were rescued from
under it. We believe one of the altar candlesticks was found
under the railway bridge on the edge of the Exe estuary.
St. Andrew's Church at Exton was a daughter Church to
Woodbury, and by the kindness of the Vicar of Woodbury
I was allowed to take the early Sunday Communion services
there from near that date. It had fallen to my lot to take the
last early Sunday service in the old building. And now I was
called upon to carry on for a year, first in the Village Hall
and then in an old tin chapel, which fortunately provided us
with temporary accommodation. Then from various sources
and liberal contributions a new church was built, designed
by Mr. Challice. This building is excellent for light and for

sound, and being pushed back from its former low level, a good car park is provided.

Voluntary drivers kindly provided transport for me to and fro on Sunday mornings, and I went by bus to some voluntary visiting, especially on Saturdays. This was a great source of consolation amid domestic sadness. One of the voluntary Sunday drivers is no longer with us. This was Mrs. Roberts, a magistrate, whose daughter is doing wonderful work amongst coloured children in Notting Hill in London. Mrs. Roberts brought me back each Sunday, and then cooked the breakfast for my wife and looked after her needs.

During these later years of my "retirement" the circumstances of my life lent themselves to my getting on steadily with the task of completing and improving the work of building up the 100 coloured plates of wild flowers. Botanical correspondents were still sending me specimens of the rarer species, which had been on the desiderata lists. Over the whole long period of half a century 82 botanists had sent 360 specimens, which were used either for a first drawing, or for improvement of those already made. So that the remark in the Preface of the work, that it was something of a combined effort, is fully justified.

These journeys to London also gave me the opportunity of visiting my elder brothers, Charlie at Chelsea while he lived, and Arthur at Englefield Green. This further purpose made the journeys important. However, my wife's illness increasingly dominated the situation. And we now had housekeepers to help us, quite a succession of them, mostly very good and kind indeed, enabling me to continue the early Sunday service at Exton, as a regular engagement and also the visiting there.

Referring to the trips to London, one of these in March 1961 was made specially to get signatures to an appeal for funds for the publication of the work on the British Flora, because all the publishers were refusing to undertake the expense of reproducing the plates in colour. I was fortunate in obtaining the signature of the Hon. Sir David Bowes-Lyon, on behalf of the Royal Horticultural Society. He died unexpectedly in the summer of that year. The other signatures included the two heads of the Botany Department at the Natural History Museum, the Director and Scientific Officer at the Royal Botanic Gardens at Kew, and a former Director of Kew, also the President of the Ray Society, Dr. W. S. Bristowe. I mention his name because he worked hard to get my plates published. His letters to me about it cover the period 1954–63. His labours helped to produce more unanimous support for publication.

Towards the end of this period my son Patrick at Wiveliscombe, Somerset, helped me very much. He sent out letters and appeals to 250 selected people. He was instrumental in collecting altogether £1,000 from a large number of subscribers. This was a very considerable secretarial work well and efficiently fulfilled. His wife also wrote with an appeal to His Royal Highness the Duke of Edinburgh who asked to see some of the plates. And 33 of the coloured plates were sent to him in August 1963. A whole year intervened before these efforts led to success. More than a year later the influence of His Royal Highness proved an immense help.

Throughout 1962 the Sunday duty continued and the visiting. This last sometimes included seeing sick members in hospital. I went to see a man in hospital on 4 December and met with an infection, which was soon pronounced shingles. And as I continued to work against this it became very severe. I was out of action for three months. I still have what I call my "pack of hounds", which are sometimes in full cry!

When I got back to work the summer of 1963 had its sorrows. My brother Arthur died, and not many days later my younger brother Dick passed from us. A little later my dear wife died suddenly while in a wheel-chair in the garden; she was facing the flowers which she could not see, for she was quite blind. This occurred in the presence of myself and my two daughters.

Near the dates of these sad events came the consecrations of two churches I had been much connected with. St. Luke's, Milber, designed by my brother Arthur, was consecrated a fortnight before he died. And St. Andrew's, Exton, was dedicated on 28 September. This was where I was ministering. It has a well-kept garden and a car park outside, most useful nowadays.

But my own home life became forlorn. I wished for more friendly companionship. The two things that helped to keep me going were the church work and the flower painting. I was doing all I could at both of these. They were like the two hand rails that we have in our bungalow, helping to keep old folk steady. I am much indebted to the kindness of the Vicar of Woodbury, the Rev. A. E. Osmond, for his kindness in allowing me to visit a part of his parish.

For this visiting I kept careful abbreviated records. I have done this all my life. It enables me to use common sense in visiting, and to pray intelligently for householders, which I am convinced has led to real and useful guidance. Nowadays patience is required in finding men at home, but it is very rewarding work, and leads to some frank discussions. If they forget to turn off the television promptly, the naughty padre stands with his back to it to talk.

In the flower painting I had arrived at the stage of improving more of the plates, re-drawing those which were on poor quality paper, or those which required adjustment in the spacing of figures. Also now that the names were agreed by the International Botanical Congress, more than 200 scientific names which were used formerly in this country, had to be washed out on the plates, and replaced by the agreed International names.

* LATER YEARS

In the spring of 1964 Mrs. Florence Lewis, a widow lady
who lived at East Horsley in Surrey, saw much of a special
friend who was dying of cancer. Mrs. Lewis was of a South
Devon family and had friends here. She was much distressed
by the death of her friend. And she wanted to get away for
a complete change, but not to do nothing. She was a keen
church member of the sort that must be working for somebody. She thought that looking after an elderly padre in
Devon would be suitable. She had done very responsible
work. She had been secretary to the Director of the Institute
of Psychology during the war years, and so had singularly
wide experience of human nature. And she also had friends
amongst the clergy.

Mrs. Lewis came at the end of April and I soon learned
to appreciate her personality. It was no wonder that she
seemed to have such a lot of good friends. She was always
writing nice letters to them, or going to see them. She had
nice ideas for the bungalow too, and produced excellent
meals. She was just quietly always at work, genuine, kindly
and trustworthy. It was not long before I said to my daughter
Lisette: "She just suits me." But I was very anxious that she
should feel free. So she visited Newquay and Horsley that
summer. I was often taken to Exton Church by a kind voluntary driver. But in July this lady sold her car to Mrs. Lewis,
who drove me after that. Our mutual behaviour was polite
and excellent, quite above reproach. No doubt mutual understanding was growing.

During the late summer I was working hard at the repainting of some of my plates of British wild flowers. At this time
33 of these plates had been at Buckingham Palace since
August 1963. So on 11 August 1964 I wrote to Squadron-
Leader Checketts to ask if there had been any result. He
replied that there had been no result whatever until yester-

day. Mr. Hadfield, Mr. George Rainbird's editor, had taken the plates to a meeting of their directors. We were told afterwards that he showed them at the meeting, and they said that they were just what was wanted. Then on 4 September, I was at my son's house at Wiveliscombe, Somerset, and Mr. George Rainbird came and talked at some length about the flower plates. He said: "Every schoolboy will want a copy." Then for many weeks to come, indeed throughout all that winter, Mr. Rainbird and his staff kept us busy with correspondence and visits, making many small corrections and adaptations to the *Concise British Flora*, as it was now called.

Meanwhile, my church work at Exton continued. But during October, I found myself considering whether I had fulfilled my duty to my children. I had spent my capital funds on their education. I had laid up my lifelong savings for them under a marriage settlement. Then on 26 October after breakfast I suddenly proposed to Mrs. Lewis. And I met the prompt reply: "Oh no, I like the name Lewis, besides I should be ruined", i.e. financially. In spite of this proposal there was no great change. Mrs. Lewis did ask at intervals: "Did I not regret what I had said?" But I always replied: "No, certainly not." I had no reason to regret it. And our polite and reserved way of life continued. We were certainly not in any hurry to part company.

Then on 5 December, Mr. Rainbird sent a telegram which was 'phoned in advance of delivery. This announced that no other than His Royal Highness Prince Philip was going to write a Foreword to my *Concise British Flora*. In the joy and excitement of the moment Mrs. Lewis forgot her reserve and threw her arms round me. So there we were! Darby and Joan, thinking alike and happy! Our intention to be married was announced for 27 January, to take place at Powderham Church, and from my youngest daughter's house there.

During the weeks of preparation we visited one another's families, travelling to Horsley in Surrey, and to Guildford for a wedding ring (I did not lose it this time), and we visited our family lawyers. I was preparing to convey the bungalow "Broadymead" to my future wife, to ensure that she would be able to live there, that place of happy memories, after my sojourn in this pilgrimage had ended.

The wedding took place in Powderham Church on the morning of 27 January 1965. We both had the idea that it was providentially planned for us. My wife's name being Florence (i.e. Florentia—Flowering One), my family and numerous relations call her "Flora". A most suitable interpretation. I gave to my wife for a wedding present the original coloured drawings of the *Concise British Flora*. What greater proof of my devotion could I give? We had nice weather for the wedding, and a reception was held by the kindness of the Whitneys at Mellands. Then in the afternoon my stepson and his wife drove us to Salisbury. We entertained them to dinner, and they then left for Horsley. The next day in snow showers we drove to Marlborough, and then to Oxford, visiting places that I had been connected with. Parking accommodation in Oxford was inadequate, and the car had to be left at the roadside. When we went to the Cathedral early on Sunday the car was covered with ice.

Finally we drove to Horsley, where I met more of my new relations and friends, 27 of them in 15 days! And I scratched a little in the garden there. But I dashed down by train for one Sunday at Exton and back again. After that we drove down at the end of the week, because I was anxious to maintain my small amount of church work.

The date of the publication of the *Concise British Flora* was now drawing near. And the British Broadcasting Corporation seemed to foresee its popularity. And in the daffodil time of spring Mr. Kenneth Allsop and some assistants came to Broadymead, Woodbury, for a whole day, taking photographs, and getting conversation out of us to make a film. So on 6 April we rather unwillingly appeared in a television programme called "Tonight". I told some of these photographers that I had never been able to afford either the time

or the money for television, and was never likely to be able
to do so. Watching it seems to be just doing nothing for
anybody. But it probably increased the sale of the *Concise
British Flora*. And Mr. Kenneth Allsop was very kind about
it.

After the early service on 2 May, we left by car for Salisbury and Horsley in order to be near London. Mr. George
Rainbird had produced a large library edition of the *Concise
British Flora*. This was on hand-made paper. And it had a
beautiful binding with tiny blue flowers impressed in white
leather, made only in springtime at Auvergne in France. He
kindly gave us a copy of this and copies to our children. And
he was granted an audience with His Royal Highness Prince
Philip along with my wife and myself in order to present a
copy to His Royal Highness and to get his signature to our
copy. This was on 6 May at Buckingham Palace, and was a
very happy occasion. It was at 12 noon, just at the time of the
changing of the guard, the band of the Welsh Guards striking
up as we arrived. His Royal Highness was very kind and was
inquiring after a smaller edition, which could be carried on
walks, and so make the expeditions of young people more
interesting.

After this Mr. and Mrs. Rainbird kindly entertained us to
luncheon, and then took us to the Lime Grove Studio to see
a repeat of the television interview at Woodbury, which Mr.
Rainbird had missed. We returned to Horsley, and a week
later we saw the beautiful Azaleas in full bloom at Wisley,
before driving back to Woodbury. The *Concise British Flora*
was published on 10 May, 1965.

At the end of May we went to Newquay for a few days'
rest from housekeeping and visitors, but at Newquay we met
with a north-east wind and rain. The beach was deserted. So
we went across to the South Cornish coast near St. Just in
Roseland. And there we found the birds singing in the
sheltered scrub on the cliffs, including white-throats, black-
caps, and willow wrens. These are just some of the birds that

have disappeared from our lane at Woodbury in recent years.

During this first summer of our newly married life we were both kept very busy, while the *Concise British Flora* was being sold out at a surprising pace. We were also still meeting more friends of both our families. And a number of people came to talk about the book, or to get their copies signed. A happy aspect of this was that kind letters were received from people that I had met in every place that I had worked in during my long ministry, even for instance from people I had christened in my first parish, or from little boys whom I had persuaded to join the church choir more than 50 years ago, who were now grandfathers and retired. This was also a period of more church work. The visiting at Exton was persevered with, and the early service there on Sundays. This was frequently followed by taking services at other churches, especially at Woodbury Salterton where the Vicar was ill. So I was preparing sermons again, and I opened a fête at Combe-in-Teignhead. And my wife opened one at Aylesbeare very ably.

Early the following January we received an invitation from Messrs. Hatchards to attend a reception to be given by them at the Martini Terrace on the sixteenth floor of New Zealand House, so we went up to Surrey by train, and then stayed at a London hotel for this great event.

Messrs. Hatchards' reception was a wonderful occasion. From the Martini Terrace we had a marvellous view of the lights of London. It was specially interesting because, owing to the phenomenal sale of the *Concise British Flora*, which made it the best seller for 1965, I was the special "Author of the Year". We met many interesting authors, booksellers and publishers. I was overwhelmed by flattery. But to use the words of the Press: "booksey success was not likely to spoil me". And I must confess I enjoyed every minute of it. On arrival, after greeting our hosts and hostesses, my wife and I were asked to sit and chat, whilst a television film was made. We did not see it afterwards but by a curious coinci-

A sample of moss prints made in 1895 from the shadows of mosses thrown by candlelight. The leaves are models

Postage stamps designed by the author in December 1966 and issued in April 1967

The Rev. W. Keble Martin
blessing his home, 1967

The Rev. and Mrs. Keble
Martin on his 90th birthday,
8 June 1967

On Hay Tor, Dartmoor,
June 1967

dence my son-in-law heard from relatives in New Zealand
that they had seen it during a morning programme some
days later. What a wonderful medium for keeping people out
there up to date with what happens in this country. A doctor
in a lonely place in Australia, when he heard that more than
a hundred thousand copies of the *Concise British Flora* had
been sold in the first year, wrote to say: "There was some
hope for humanity after all', and a padre in Southern England
wrote similar words.

During this spring (1966), the second year of publication,
I was invited by Exeter University to attend their Degree
Day to be held on 30 June to receive the honorary degree of
Doctor of Science. I agreed. So the necessary scarlet robes
were prepared. When the time came my wife and I attended
a University dinner party on 29 June. The other guest of
honour was Miss Margaret Digby, O.B.E., Secretary of the
Plunket Foundation. And then on Degree Day, 30 June, after
a laudatory speech by the public orator, Dr. Clayton, the
degree of Doctor of Science was conferred by the Chancellor
of the University, the Dowager Duchess of Devonshire. And
then it was interesting to see some hundreds of young people
passing before me to receive their several degrees. The
ceremony was followed for us by a family luncheon at the
Imperial Hotel, completing this happy occasion.

During this second year after the publication of the *Concise
British Flora* we were kept very busy with callers and letters,
more than could be answered. Some limited church work continued, especially the little bit of visiting, with some interesting discussions, also the early service on Sundays at Exton.
The preaching was disappointingly rare, only at Drewsteignton and Gidleigh and once suddenly at Exton. There was also
the opening of a Church fête at Milber, all these amongst
old friends.

The two families, Martin and Lewis, saw more of one
another, exchanging visits. My wife and I went twice for
short visits to my youngest daughter's new home in North

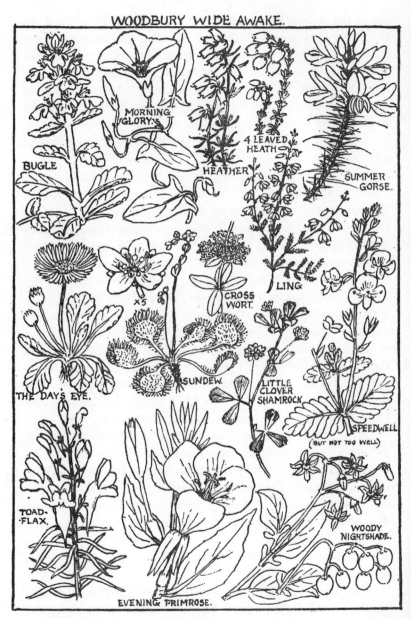

Cover for the *Woodbury News*, August 1966, designed by the author

Devon, and for a brief stay at Patrick's home at Wiveliscombe. We paid four visits to Horsley to see more of my
wife's friends. And her son Geoffrey and his wife sometimes
stayed at Woodbury. Twice he drove us down from Surrey.
He also took us for wonderful country drives that year, to
Fingle Bridge at daffodil time, and to East Hill to see the
bluebells, also to Shipley Bridge near Brent, and another day
to Clovelly. My wife drove me to Torrington, where I met
old friends. So we had a gay time of rushing about.

In the autumn I was celebrating Holy Communion one
weekday at Exton (St. Simon and St. Jude's Day, 28 October),
and when I came out of the church, I was suddenly informed
that the Postmaster-General had said on the radio that he
was asking me to paint some stamps with wild flower designs.
I heard direct three days later. There were no wild flowers
to paint at that season. But I had the advantage of being
allowed by the publisher to adapt drawings from the *Concise
British Flora*. The designs were to be completed by 12
December. So partly at Woodbury and partly at Horsley I
worked hard at this. On some days the light was too weak
for me to see the colours properly by 2 p.m. So we had to
rise early and use the forenoon. The stamps were to be
printed at Messrs. Harrison's Stamp Printing Works at High
Wycombe. And Mr. York, director of Harrisons, kindly invited us to visit the printing works. So we were shown all over
that wonderful place by Mr. Gray. This was rather a thrilling
experience. My own designs were completed at Woodbury,
and were dispatched to Messrs. Harrison's to be completed
with the addition of the Queen's head on 5 December.

After posting the stamp designs, there was a busy period
of church work and visiting in preparation for Christmas. My
wife also was very busy with preparations for the festival,
sending out about a hundred Christmas cards, decorating the
house and welcoming the family to wonderful meals. I was
also preparing another great-nephew for Confirmation and
later presenting him for this at Holy Trinity Church in

Exmouth. There was a brief visit between Sundays to Horsley, and a very short one to my daughter's house in North Devon.

But in the middle of February 1967, we were suddenly called to Surrey again. My wife and I were invited by the Postmaster-General to a Press Conference on 22 February. This was followed by a luncheon with him at the Post Office Tower. The Tower has a marvellous restaurant at the top with an ever-changing bird's-eye view of London. This was indeed a memorable occasion. Mr. Short, the Postmaster-General, was very kind and hospitable to us. And we met, amongst others, Miss Mary Grierson, the Kew artist, who was the other successful stamp designer.

During April we were away for longer. We were kindly invited by Messrs. Hatchards to another reception for authors, publishers and booksellers at New Zealand House on 5 April. This was because the *Concise British Flora* was still among the best sellers. And then we stayed in Surrey until after the issue of the stamps on 24 April. I had many requests to sign stamps and first day covers. And we were told that Westward Television showed a queue of local boys calling at Broadymead in Woodbury, to have their stamps signed on the first day, but we were away.

During this spring and early summer we were being made a fuss of by friends and family and neighbours, and even by people unknown to us hitherto, bringing books or stamps to be signed. It is a curious feature of human nature that when one is known for something done, the people we visit are more willing to give attention to anything we say. If this happens we are surely responsible for making use of it.

At the beginning of June we had a well-earned rest at Holne Chase on the River Dart and we were able to visit many beautiful spots and favourite haunts. We had some delightful walks, climbing Hay Tor and Buckland Beacon.

Four days after our return I was taken very seriously ill. I caused my wife grave anxiety, but owing to her loving care

and prompt action, I found myself in Budleigh Salterton
Hospital, though I do not remember going there. I had the
benefit of the best medical skill and excellent nursing for
which I am very grateful. And I was able to leave the hospital
in time for my 90th birthday, 9 July. Although I was still far
from strong my family and friends made this a very festive
occasion, friends to sherry, and then my own family to tea.
The house was gay with cards and telegrams, also flowers
and fruit, and even beautiful books. A special happiness had
been receiving unexpectedly the first copy of the Dutch edition
of the *Concise British Flora*. This was flown over specially to
give me a wonderful surprise, while I was still very ill in
hospital. Meanwhile my wife has done wonderful work. Her
efforts and prayers have given me a new lease of life, and
enabled me among other things to write this story.

And so, in my ninety-first year, I look back on a happy and
busy life. I celebrated Holy Communion again after an inter-
val of two months and I hope to continue yet. I trust not only
that my ministry has been helpful, but also that many young
people, and those not so young, will be inspired by the *Concise
British Flora* to recognize and love the wild flowers, to roam
over the moors and mountains and seasides, discovering for
themselves the wealth of flowers in our beautiful country.
They would find it a healthy interest which they would never
regret.

A Naturalist's View
of the
Old Testament
and the
Gospels

The Old Testament Scriptures

We have in the world only one intimate picture of the life of an early people, namely of Israel. That history is scattered through the books of the Old Testament Scriptures. Much is now known from other sources about the peoples of Western Asia in the period covered by Israel's history, the rise and fall of empires, and the way in which they lived. And the picture in the Bible fits in with it. It is thoroughly typical of that life. The campaigns of these powers can now be traced and approximately dated. Indeed many of the events recorded in the Bible are mentioned in secular records. The general picture is thoroughly true to life.

But there was one very important difference. The other nations were without the belief in one God of Holiness. They even pictured spiritual powers quarrelling together over the creation of an evil world. They worshipped many gods. They worshipped the sun. Their king was often one of their gods. They had not that help to righteous living, which was to come from faith in one God of Holiness, the creator of all.

It is quite true that the records in the Bible seem rather fragmentary. They have passed through translation into different languages and scripts. This has produced some errors of translation, secondly, the copyists have made mistakes.

But the books are based on earlier records in the form of clay tablets, as well as on very strong oral tradition, which was most carefully taught, and deliberately passed on from one generation to another. In spite of disadvantages of a human kind the history in the Bible is a record of what God has done to make known his work and his will for mankind and to bring mankind into personal contact with him, a relation of responsibility, friendship and love.

The earliest picture of the "scientific" ideas current in Babylon, which is given us on contemporary clay tablets, shows us that this side of it is followed in the Bible picture, which is not given to us as a short cut to science. God gives that in another way. * But the Bible picture completely changes the heathen character of the original. Abraham was living amongst heathen people and perhaps it is true, as an early writer says, that he was persecuted for his faith. He thought that God called upon him to migrate to Syria, and he obeyed. Tradition pictured Abraham as the "friend of God". "He trusted in God and it was counted to him for righteousness."

We now follow the teaching of a learned but conservative writer† in saying that the language of records in Mesopotamia from which Abraham came was Babylonian Cuneiform, inscribed with a stylus on clay tablets, which were usually afterwards baked and which were very permanent. Enormous quantities of them have been found. This was long before Hebrew came into use. And we believe that Abraham was himself responsible for inscribing clay tablets giving the picture of Creation in the first chapter of Genesis. It was, like the traditions that follow, in the scientific ideas of Babylon but saying truly that "God created the heavens and the earth, and God saw that it was good".

Nature is good, beautiful and happy. Only personality can

---

* See page 52.

† Dr. E. Navilles' "Schweich Lecture" on the *Text of the Old Testament*, to the British Academy 1916. Published by the Oxford University Press.

make or appreciate beauty. "And God created Man in his own likeness", that is personal and responsible to him. In fact that Man was made for this personal friendship and loving response to God. Men are to be "Workers together with Him". This results in the traditions of his family that also follow in Genesis, but the Syriac version adds another hundred years to the ages of each of the patriarchs to magnify their importance, revealing a prevalent weakness of copyists.

The books of the Exodus onwards are traditionally pictured as the work of Moses. They claim repeatedly to have been so. In fact modern scholars have pointed out that not some unknown writers of 600 years later but *Moses* was the only known man, who could possibly have composed those pictures. He alone had that full knowledge of the life of Egypt and the Court of the Pharaohs, and also of the intimate pathetic story of Joseph and the family of Israel. At the end of the last century it was the custom of scholars to break up these stories almost verse by verse, and attribute them severally to the priests or to the schools of the Prophets according to which divine name was used in Hebrew. But these nice stories in Exodus etc. were written long before the existence of Hebrew writing, and no man of Ezra's time could have had the knowledge required. Moses is pictured as a man of humility but was always regarded as the true prophet of God. It is from prayer and solitude on the mountain that he comes to give them God's law. We believe that he was inspired to inscribe the law with a stylus in wedge-shaped letters on soft clay, which had to be baked, and that these tablets had been most carefully preserved in exile, and allowed to return like the vessels of the temple, and that they must have been in the hands of Ezra.

This main teaching of Moses includes the Ten Commandments. God is one and is holy. We are to worship him. We are not to worship any golden image. (Do we worship money today?) We are to reverence God, his Holy Name. We are to set aside one day in seven for rest and worship. And in

regard to our neighbour, we are to have a friendly, trustworthy relation to all, producing mutual confidence. Personal
response to God and to our neighbour. That is God's will
for us.

At a much later date came the *Former Prophets*. In the
schools of the prophets from the time of Samuel the history
of God's people is similarly recorded from the point of view
of their personal response to the will of God. They either
"were righteous in the sight of the Lord" or "they did evil
in the sight of the Lord". Then came the *Later Prophets*.
The great writing prophets were God's men. They were
personally in touch with God through prayer. He inspired
them to speak for him, and they nearly always suffered for
their witness to him. The people of Israel were indeed called
to faith in One Holy God. God is thought of as the Shepherd
of his people. Human shepherds have dangerous work. There
are still wolves in Palestine of a large variety that hunt singly.
How would you like to meet one alone at break of day?

God was thought of as the Shepherd of his people. They
were "the sheep of his pasture". Or he was the Lord of his
vineyard. "What could have been done more to my vineyard
that I have not done in it?" The prophets foretold that a
fuller, more personal revelation would come from God
through the Messiah.

Now a strange thing happened. It was God's will. Just as
the seed of corn has to be scattered or spread on the land. So
this faith in God and expectation of fuller revelation was
widely sown in the world by the scattering of Israel two or
three centuries before Christ came. That dispersion was
always called "diaspora", i.e. "the scattering of the seed".
The occasion of the scattering of Israelites is in many cases
known in history or recorded in Scripture, but the extent of
it was so great that about a third of the population in many
big cities of the Roman Empire were either Israelites or their
converts from other nations. In all countries of the known
world they were in vast numbers, literally millions. And they

won many to faith in the One Holy God. And so many travelled to Jerusalem for the great feasts that the historian Josephus asserts that more than 2½ million came to Jerusalem. The Roman Empire had made travelling easy, levelling boundaries, making good roads everywhere. In addition to this the Greek language, the language of education, was equally spreading. The Scriptures had been translated into Greek.

The Prophets had borne witness to the holiness of God and had suffered for it. They had foretold that God would give a fuller revelation in the Messiah (*Messiah* means the *anointed* one, *Christos* the Christ means the same. The anointing of prophets, priests and kings was the symbol of giving the Holy Spirit). These four things, the forecast of the prophets, the dispersion of those who believed it, the opening of boundaries and roads, and the widespread unity of language did indeed prepare the way for faith in Christ the Holy One of God. Referring to the preparatory work our Lord said to his apostles: "Lift up your eyes and look on the fields, they are white already for harvest. Others have laboured and ye are entered into their labours." Although Jewish leaders in many cases expected a worldly deliverer and jealously resisted Christianity, they could not stop its spreading, neither could persecution by the government which demanded the worship of the Emperor.

"The fulness of time had come (Gal. 4, 4) God sent forth his Son." "He who spake unto the fathers by the prophets hath in these last days spoken unto us by his Son" (Heb. 1, 1–2). The full revelation of the meaning and responsibility of human life, and the demonstration of Divine love had to be made *within* human personality, and it involved the greatest sacrifice of love. There was no alternative. "The good shepherd must lay down his life for the sheep."

A few thoughts about the first three Gospel writers, who have often been discussed in our recent visiting.

1. *St. Matthew's Gospel*

Early traditions agree in saying that Matthew wrote down many of "the sayings" of Jesus the "ipsissima verba" in the local Aramaic language. The sayings were called in the Greek "Ta Logia". And it seems to have been just because Matthew in due course extended his writing into a "Gospel" that the expression "Ta Logia" became used for the "Gospel". We do not doubt that the earliest tradition is correct, and that Matthew was the writer of "Ta Logia" in both senses.

So we can turn to the internal evidence of the Gospel itself. Here was a young man, who was brought up in the thorough knowledge of the Old Testament Scriptures in the Greek or Septuagint version, which he quoted quite freely. He was filled by this knowledge with keen expectation of the coming of the Messiah. And there is in this Gospel a note of triumphant joy in recording the fulfilment of prophecy. Jesus was the King Messiah of Israel.

When the ministry of Christ began Matthew was posted to a place of toll at Capernaum on the main road from Damascus to Acre on the coast. He examined goods carried on the road, and he levied toll either for Herod or for Imperial funds. For his business he had to use both the Greek and Aramaic languages, and he was accustomed to writing. The travellers on the roads were almost the only carriers of news in those days. Nazareth was near a main road about twenty miles away. It is usual to suppose that the Birth stories of the Christ in this Gospel represent just the current belief of Christians in Palestine. But this does not explain the intimate picture of the thoughts of Joseph, or the addition of a family pedigree of his ancestry. This rather suggests the entrusting of a written account.

Matthew was collecting taxes at Capernaum; such men

could easily enrich themselves. Jesus stayed there in Capernaum twice. Evidently Matthew was a keen listener. Jesus called Matthew to follow him, and Matthew promptly left his money-making business and followed Christ. He also gathered his publican friends to meet the Christ.

The "sayings" of Jesus which Matthew recorded are a main feature of the Gospel, where they are grouped together. The first and longest group is the Sermon on the Mount as we call it, in chapters 5–7, with the wonderful beatitudes, the teaching about prayer and about trust in God. In your work "serve God not mammon, not money". If you serve God you will not want. "Behold the birds (skylarks, gold crests, robins, etc.). Your Heavenly Father feedeth them." "Consider the lilies, how beautiful, God so clothes them." The "sayings" also include his instruction to the disciples, when he sent them out (chap. 10), also a group of parables (chap. 13). Parables of the sower and the soil, of the good seed and the tares, and of the fishing net. The "sayings" also include some rules of humility and forgiveness (chap. 18) and warnings of judgement (chap. 24–25). In this last the forecast of the destruction of Jerusalem is rather mixed up with the picture of the end of the world, showing that the final editing of the Gospel must be dated before the destruction of Jerusalem in AD 70.

This Gospel is written from a very strongly Jewish Christian point of view. The Birth stories and all represent the belief among Christians in Palestine, about the middle of the first century and all is in fulfilment of Old Testament prophecy. Jesus is the expected *Messiah King* of Israel. The writer makes much of Peter's leadership. And so he seems to include a large part of Mark's Gospel, i.e. Peter's Gospel, possibly an early recension of it. It is the fashion among scholars to say that the final editing of this Gospel was not done by Levi Matthew. The reasons are not obvious to ordinary folk. In any case this makes no difference. Tradition is agreed about the "sayings" being those of Our Lord.

Repeated study of the long accounts in the Dictionary of the
Gospels and elsewhere has not altered our opinion. We think
of St. Paul as divinely inspired to teach the wider meaning
of Our Lord's Incarnation and ministry. It was necessary
for God's will and love to be revealed within human personality. This involved suffering for us and now what we
call Christmas, Good Friday, Easter and Ascension Day.

2. St. Mark's Gospel

A young man who lived in one of the largest houses in
Jerusalem had perhaps recently completed his education. His
name was John Mark. His mother listened to the wonderful
teaching of the Christ. And she offered to Him the use of
the large Upper Room in her house for the Passover Feast
with his disciples. But there was a traitor, and *he* must not
know where the Feast was to be held. So she agreed to send
her son to the fountain just at sunset to meet two disciples,
and lead them to the Upper Room. At the fountain he beckons
to them with his hand to follow, and he leads them to the
Upper Room, where they made the necessary preparation.
After his own supper with his mother young John Mark
retired to bed. But towards midnight a lot of armed men
came to the door demanding admission with authority of the
High Priest. The young man and his mother perceive what
is intended. So he runs lightly clad to warn the Christ. But
he does not find him until the moment of the betrayal in the
Garden of Gethsemane. Even so he tries to approach the
Christ, but the armed men snatched at him, and tore most of
his light attire off him. The young man could never forget
this little effort to help. And when much later on he is writing
Peter's sermons and translating them, he inserts this little
story of his own experience.

The friendship with Peter was caused by his experience of
this Upper Room. When Peter was released from prison he
came to that house, "the house of Mary, the mother of Mark"

where many were gathered together praying and in the days that followed Peter was probably teaching Mark about Christ. Peter called him "Markus my son". John Mark's mother had a brother, Joseph Barnabas, a Levite of Cyprus, who sold his land near Jerusalem and gave the proceeds to the Church. He introduced Saul after his conversion to the Apostles, and later on it was again Barnabas who brought Saul from Tarsus to Antioch to preach. So this family did important work. Joseph Barnabas was a good man full of the Holy Ghost.

When Paul and Barnabas had come to Jerusalem on an errand of mercy they took young Mark, Barnabas' nephew, back with them to Antioch, and a little later when they went on their first missionary journey, they again took Mark with them to Cyprus as a helper, indeed Barnabas twice took him to Cyprus, with which the family was connected. But on the first occasion Mark was not ready to follow to the mainland on missionary journeys to foreigners. He was young, and the first time at least he returned to his mother's house in Jerusalem, where he came again under the influence of Peter, completing his training. The friendship of Peter and Mark became deep and fruitful.

St. Mark's Gospel in its final form must have been written not later than about AD 64.

Eusebius in his history quotes Bishop *Papias* of Hierapolis, AD 136, saying: "Mark having become the interpreter of Peter, wrote down accurately everything that Peter related" about Christ. That is, Mark translated Peter's narrative from Aramaic into Greek, probably also into Latin at Rome. This translation was his life's work. There are half a dozen Latin words (like "Centurion") in St. Mark's Gospel. Other early writers confirm this. *Irenaeus*, Bishop of Lyons 120–200, is very definite: "Mark handed on to us in writing the things preached by Peter." That is to say Mark's Gospel is in effect Peter's Gospel. Clement of Alexandria (about AD 190) says that while Peter was preaching the Gospel at Rome, many of those present begged Mark to write down what Peter said. Origen, also of Alexandria (200–230), says that "Mark wrote the Gospel at Peter's instruction". What an important work this ordinary young man fulfilled!

So we find that St. Mark's Gospel begins when Peter first met our Lord, and is limited to Peter's own experience of him. It gives a very vivid picture, evidently of an eyewitness of many scenes, recording points like the glance, or the effect of words spoken, and omits stress on Peter's own importance. It is written in simple, rather crude, language. The greater part of it is taken both by Matthew and Luke into their Gospels. But both, especially Luke, softened some of the crude expressions used by Mark. Thus St. Mark's Gospel gives us a vivid picture of Peter's human experience of Christ, the Messiah, the Son of God. There can be no doubt about Peter's faith in the *Son of God* become *Man*. He tells how they realized at Caesarea Philippi that He was the Messiah (8, 41) and records Our Lord's teaching that this involved His going through suffering to Glory. "He shall come in glory." So for Peter, Christ is "the Holy One of God" (1, 24) "the Beloved Son" (11, 11; 9, 7) "with supernatural authority and miraculous power, Lord of the Sabbath" (2, 28) the "Forgiver of sins" (2, 5–10). His coming in future glory (8, 38; 14, 61–62). But it shows especially Peter's own personal relation to his Lord. The last leaf of Mark's Gospel was lost, and another hand supplied the last 16 verses early in the second century. The better picture is supplied in Peter's own words in his undoubted first Epistle, chapter 1. "Blessed be the God and Father of Our Lord Jesus Christ, who according to his great mercy hath begotten us again into a living hope by the Resurrection of Jesus Christ from the dead" etc. He had denied his Lord, and had been forgiven by the risen Lord.

It is probable that Mark was for several years helping Peter by translating his preaching and that to write down what he was usually translating was a help to him. So there were portions of his Gospel written earlier, earlier recensions of his Gospel.

3. St. Luke's Gospel

In our many talks about St. Luke we have regarded him from the point of view of Dr. R. B. Rackham in his *Acts of the Apostles*. This work is widely read and has been reprinted thirteen times.

He regards St. Luke, Dr. Lucanus, as of an aristocratic Greek family, which came from Philippi, but which had settled in Antioch in Pisidia. He was a medical man but well read. He knew the works of the Greek poets, and uses some 750 words, which occur in no other New Testament writer. From Pisidian Antioch he probably visited Tarsus and met St. Paul and was converted to Christianity. His character was indeed one of Christian joy and love.

Luke apparently accompanied Paul and Barnabas, to Antioch in Syria, when Barnabas went to seek Paul. This was probably AD 42. Luke is at once able to throw clear light on the Church at Syrian Antioch. According to the earliest Bezan text* of the Acts we read (11, 28): "There was much rejoicing, and when we were gathered together there stood up one named Agabus." Luke entirely effaces himself in his writings. He appears to have accompanied Paul on his first missionary journey. Paul needed the doctor. Perhaps he had shingles, with lasting pain in the eyes (Gal. 4, 13–15). This journey has a singularly graphic narrative, e.g. "St. Paul stood up and beckoned with his hand" (Acts 13–14, AD 46–47). He was also probably on the second missionary journey (AD 49, Acts 15, 36–18, 22). After the vision of the man of Macedonia we sailed and came to Philippi. In 54 he probably went at Paul's request on a mission to Corinth (2 Cor. 8, 18). In the

---

* The soundest explanation of the longer Bezan Text of Acts is that Luke shortened it himself to fit the parchments, omitting many sentences that were unnecessary, but also further effacing himself by omitting the "we" clause above.

6

spring probably of 55 he joined Paul on his final journey to Jerusalem. And he stayed in Palestine for two years. This was quite important.

Christian love was the basis of St. Luke's character. He was "the beloved physician". He entirely effaces his own share in the work. He often records the joy of the Christian community. In the first part, the Acts of Peter (Acts 1–12), he does not mention any dates. He had none, but, in the second part regarding Paul, he is very exact in his record of the intervals of time.

Luke was familiar with the officials of Judaism, and with all the changing officials of the many little states visited on the missionary journeys in Asia Minor, etc. We are assured by Dr. Rackham that in all this intricacy "Luke was never caught tripping".* The names and titles are all correct. He was formerly thought to be mistaken about "the politarchs of Thessalonica" and the "proconsul of Cyprus", but the modern discovery of inscriptions has proved him correct. He was the safest historian of that important century. He knew also that the secret of human history lies in human personality. His own truly human character gives him a deep insight into the characters he depicts. He was faithful to the end. St. Paul in his last letter says: "Only Luke is with me." It had become dangerous in Rome to be a Christian (2 Tim. 4, 11). So much for Luke's personality.

St. Luke had great advantages. First he had a truly Christian character and he had above most people the ability to read characters and to depict them beautifully in his writing. He had also two other great advantages, first of having listened continually to Paul's preaching and secondly of being placed now for two years in Palestine, alternately helping Paul and then searching out the Christians, those who had been "eyewitnesses", and ministering to them.

Luke is thought to have had a good deal of contact with St. John as he uses many similar expressions. St. John had a

* Rackham's *Acts of Apostles*, p. 45.

house in Jerusalem, and records the commending of the Blessed Mother to his care. Picture what must have followed the Resurrection and the gift of the Holy Spirit (Acts 3–4, 14), St. John had very clear memory of the sayings of Jesus, and could write wonderful accounts of them. While the oral preaching was going on, were not some of the later sayings recorded, as memoranda quite soon after they were spoken? These sayings are apt to be followed in St. John's Gospel by his comments or preaching upon them, spiritual thoughts, arising from the wonderful life of the worshipping Church, and collected into the form of a Gospel many years later.

It is surely likely that while John was moved to write down items of his experience, the Blessed Mother also recorded some account of the very wonderful experience, that had been hers if indeed she had not related it long before. Dr. Lucanus was indeed the first doctor to inquire into the Virgin Birth. It is unthinkable that Luke did not seek out that house. If so he may well have seen the Blessed Mother's record of her experience. It looks as though he had translated it into Greek in the first two chapters of his Gospel. The account there appears to be so translated. It is very Semitic, full of Aramaic thoughts and expressions. It includes the beautiful inspired songs of Mary, of Zacharias and of Simeon. (Think about these songs. They came from the hearts of the singers.) And it adds the experience of the shepherds. St. Luke also is alone in recording the sermon at Nazareth.

St. Luke is pleased to find and record stories showing the wide human sympathy of Christ like that of the Good Samaritan. And he records more than others of Our Lord's treatment about penitents. The parable of the Lost Sheep is fuller and followed by that of the Lost Coin, showing that "there is joy in the presence of the Angels of God over one sinner that repenteth". The story of the "Prodigal Son" follows: his saying "Father I have sinned . . . I am no more worthy". And the father's reply to the elder brother: "It was right that we should rejoice". He records the prayers of the

Pharisee and of the Publican who says: "God be merciful to me a sinner."

We suppose that when St. Luke was in Palestine it was fully twenty years since the Crucifixion had taken place. It is not unlikely that some of those who had taken part in it had become Christians, some soldiers or the Centurion. If so this would doubtless be known in the Christian community. Were they still on military service there? Or did they stay after the service ended? It seems as though St. Luke found one of them, and that he related to him how when the three crosses were laid on the ground, and the Christ was being nailed to the Cross, they heard that quiet prayer: "Father, forgive them for they know not what they do." Then St. Luke's informants seem to correct St. Mark, and to say that only one of the malefactors railed against Christ. The other, having heard the above prayer, rebuked him. "This man hath done nothing amiss. Jesus remember me when thou comest in thy Kingdom" and Jesus' reply: "*Today* shalt thou be with *me* in Paradise." Again St. Luke alone records the last words of Jesus on the cross: "Father into thy hands I commend my spirit." Psalm 31, 6 with the word "Father" added.

The Roman historian Cornelius Tacitus was born about AD 54 and became a Consul of Rome in 97. He hated the Christians. He wrote in his Annals: "The Christians are so named after Christ who was put to death under the procurator Pontius Pilate, and this terrible superstition was suppressed, but immediately afterwards it broke out again like an eruption (*erumpebat*) in Judaea and even in Rome." So incidentally he bears witness to the effect of the Resurrection.

A university professor said to me recently: "Christianity seemed to be wonderfully suitable for human nature." He called himself an agnostic. In truth Christianity is intensely practical. If we, frail creatures that we are, honestly try to adapt our lives to the Divine Will revealed in Christ, this leads us to action; it enables and guides the action all the time.

Another who called himself a humanist, seeing the bad behaviour of young people today, did say that it rather appeared that all good was not in human life, there seemed to be need of something else, that Christians call grace.

One man said recently he wished *he* had Christian faith, another said he had been a communicant of the Church but his faith was upset by modern science, the creative powers of man are so wonderful. Are they? Man cannot make "life" of any kind, and the powers stored in nature, coal, electricity, ether, radio, have been there in creation from time unknown, and man, so little and slow, is only just finding out!

Another said: "I know you cannot *prove a negative* or that the life of our Lord was *not* all that it claims to be." But that is poor thought indeed. Rather it is the *positive* experience, both our own, if willing, and of countless thousands who have found their real life in Christ. His teaching puts human life at its best and purposeful. "Never man spake like this man." The works that he did and does still. He said truly: "The works that I do bear witness of me that the Father hath sent me." The uplifting and healing power of his personality. Personality can indeed sometimes overrule the normal sequence of events in Nature. This normal sequence is God's will for us. Lastly, his love for us knows no limit. "No man hath greater love than this that he lay down his life for his friends. Ye are my friends if ye do what I tell you."

So we each have a personal relation to him of love. He prompts us to put aside our pleasures, using common sense. But since we fail, it has to be through penitence, forgiveness and grace of renewal that we learn to serve our fellow men, for this is the happy life for us all. And let us stand up for chastity and decency in these evil days (Cor. 6, 9–10).

We are sometimes reminded that friendship and example speak louder than words. How true! The writer has been a padre for 65 years. The study required makes it hard work but happy.

Also I earnestly hope that in due course the present

shortage of ordained clergy will be overcome, that many young men will discover that the truly self-sacrificing work of the Ministry is not only useful and purposeful, but also the happiest work possible. But it does require a lot of honest study and consideration of the experience of our fellow men recorded in the Scriptures, and that we should go from this to faithful and continuous visiting, that we may pass on some of it in very friendly talks to those in our parishes. Visiting is more difficult today but doubly necessary. I long to say more but must cut it short.

INDEX

✳ Index

Figures in *italic* refer to the author's line drawings in the text